**FROM THE AUTHOR OF
'FLYPAPER FOR FREAKS'**

FREAKING HIRED!

**HOW RECRUITMENT PRACTICES
SABOTAGE HOPES AND DREAMS**

MAX FRANCES

Published by
Wordissimo
YOUR WORDS, ELEVATED.

WORDISSIMO.CO.UK

©2019 Max Frances

ISBN: 9781705841853

Author's Note

Thank you to those who appreciated my section on recruitment in the contact centre world in *Flypaper for Freaks* and wanted more of a wider-ranging exposé of recruitment as a whole. You ignited the spark of which this book is the flickering flame.

As something of a follow-up to *Flypaper for Freaks*, there are some notable differences between the two books. *Flypaper* was intended to be an all-encompassing exposé of an entire industry, namely BPO Contact Centres, albeit with ideas that would certainly be applicable to other enterprises and situations.

Freaking Hired! is about one broader domain, that is to say recruitment practices, that you will encounter wherever you go. It also does, as is my personal bent, open up the outsourced dimension.

Well, once you have them by the balls, their hearts and minds will surely follow.

As with so many areas of business in the UK, outsourcing plays an often invisible but certainly crucial role. It can also be argued that its contribution not only facilitates business but changes and even shapes it. That's certainly an argument I advance in my work.

Like *Flypaper for Freaks*, this is about highlighting processes and behaviours, not singling out perpetrators. It is nice to be important but important to be nice.

Yet as Kafka once said: *'A book must be the axe for the frozen sea within us'.*[ii]

§

I should take a moment – as I did in *Flypaper* – to say a few words about writing.

My goal is always to provide you with an informative and entertaining account of the matters at hand. Writers sometimes remain rigidly formal to the point that they sacrifice their personality or stifle their creativity in order to adhere to formal grammatical rules. Others are informal to the extreme and to the point that their work is but a collection of fragments. Sometimes both styles work to great effect, but neither approach would work for me, nor I think for you, with these kinds of subjects.

The style I have nurtured is therefore largely conventional but with some exceptions. I use contractions, which some purists would no doubt hate. I also make up words if the circumstances require it. And while I am an aficionado of punctuation, I sometimes slip in some additional commas for effect. It will annoy those who want to analyse what I've written, but my aim is to cater for those who want to read and enjoy it.

If you do spot anything particularly egregious though, please do let me know via www.maxfrances.com – I am always ready to amend and update in the name of progress and improvement.

Hearty thanks as well to those with respected careers within the recruitment industry who contributed insight even if they are not truly respected outside of it (read on further to understand why!)

Thank you also to those in the world of *Recruitment Process Outsourcing* who shone a discerning light onto the depths to which recruitment practices never fail to stoop. It was enlightening to see that *RPOs* continue to lead the race to the bottom.

Thank you to those who have taken the time to look at what I have to say on this inescapable feature of organisational life. I hope you enjoy reading *Freaking Hired!* as much as I enjoyed writing it.

Finally, I hope that it proves to be a useful document for those hoping to gain insight into recruitment in practice. After all, as Sartre says: *'Human life begins on the far side of despair'.*[iii]

MF

"People know what they do; frequently they know why they do what they do; but what they do not know is what what they do does." [iv]

Michel Foucault (1926-1984)

Contents

1 – First Words	9
2 – Avoiding the Rabbit Holes to Split Some Hares	14
3 – Blessed Are the Kingmakers	18
4 – Brigands, Not Talent!	36
5 – Your History…	45
6 – On a Role	55
7 – The External Hard Drive	61
8 – Back of the Net!	73
9 – Do Not Mention the War. I Mentioned It Once, and I Think I Got Away with It!	84
10 – Wagons Role!	109
11 – Funnel Vision	123
12 – The Psycho Matrix	135
13 – The New Black	152
14 – All Play and No Work Makes Jack	172
15 – Venn Trick or Circles?	197
16 – Panel Beating	206

17 – Hanging on the Telephone	231
18 – Video Killed the Audio Star	240
19 – Centres of Gravitas	246
20 – Is it Offer, Nothing?	252
21 – Food for Fraught	258
Endnote	271

1 – First Words

Most of us have, at one stage or another, been involved in recruitment processes. Whether as a candidate, hiring manager or assessor, we all have a story or two to tell. The whole process is always, well, quite a journey.

There have been a great number of creditable books on the subject, many of which are *how-to do* technical manuals for those in the business of recruiting.

My interest lies elsewhere.

I wanted to write something for the seemingly failing and disappointed candidates. The ones who feel inadequate after rejection. I have aimed to provide reassurance while at the same time offering some helpful pointers.

In a world where justice prevailed, that reassurance would come from the recruiters themselves and start with a clear *'It is not you; it is me'.*

Now, I have heard that many times during my life though sadly never from a recruiter(!)

So why do candidates think that the failure is always *theirs?* Well, it is a straightforward logical deduction, driven by omnipresent norms.

Everything out there screams that normalised recruitment behaviours and processes are valid and, moreover, underpinned by legal safeguards.

It has to be you because the processes and measurements are so solid and sound.

You make your application just like all other candidates in accordance with an open and shared set of rules, designed and implemented by experts. And if rejected (or *regretted* as they like to say – this connects the recruiter to a sense of sorrow for the message only, not any facts-based agreement with the decision – you have to accept that the battle was won by the better person on the day.

To suggest otherwise will stimulate the ire of the mainstream. Sour grapes and whining, to accidentally coin the pun.

Your rejection automatically acquires validity, along with your own appropriation of personal responsibility. You feel failure because we are taught that in the absence of injustice and obvious errors from others, we all have to take responsibility for what we do. And any failure in a recruitment process is always taken to be automatically the result of what *we* do.

Now I am not so entitled that I see failure as something that I should never experience. Far from it. Like many (but not all), at times not quite hitting the mark is to be expected in life. We cannot be experts at all endeavours and naturally, the desire to improve is what helps us to plough on and to make progress. Without it, life would arguably be somewhat dull.

Which is all fine and dandy as long as we are all on a level playing field. Unfortunately, in matters recruitment, I do not think we are.

§

Well, I am going to help you see the light. Not trying to sell you any product or course. Not trying to recruit you into a cult. Just to see it all for what it is and hopefully to help you onto a different track.

At the very least, I hope that I can help you see that, while you are not perfect, you are actually ok. That life can be a challenge, but that you really do not need these tossers to make you feel any worse. And to help you understand that what you may have been taking as your failure, *may well have been that of others.*

I refer to them as tossers because that's what a lot of them are. Sociopathic tossers. Which is a shame for the majority of people out there who are not, but who seem to fall under the spell and control of the warped minority.

The problem with recruitment is that it straddles the most important two elements of modern life: people and the means to live. And hell do they ever leverage it. And it is what keeps us all on a leash because we have to engage in the games in order to get from A to B.

If we cannot master those games, these unfair and skewed processes limit opportunity, progress, and social mobility. Not easy, when it is often impossible to work out which game is being played. Surely everything should be about working hard, boosting knowledge and sharpening skills, with the result that you get hired for being the best person for the job. That would seem to be the fairest context and is the one that is the putative underbelly of recruitment processes.

Nothing could however be further from the truth.

Yet, while right-minded folk are keen to take up the cudgels when faced with overt moves to promulgate inequality, particularly those that carry extremist tinges, process-driven inequity seems to pass merrily under the societal radar.

It is as if the dissent falls away as long as everybody is nice about it. That a coup – as long as it is peaceful – will equate to a democracy.

Have we forgotten why, in law, we have protections against indirect as well as direct discrimination? Well, for me, you can look at the issues in recruitment in a similar way. The ultimate harm created is the same for many as if it had always been the deliberate intention in the first instance.

I am hoping that I can break down the components so that some light is shed on the underlying mechanics and so that you can internalise this and re-set your perspectives.

Perhaps you will be able to alleviate some personal burden when your next application goes pear-shaped. You might even develop better coping strategies. At the very least I hope this makes you feel a greater sense of self-worth and helps you *to take back control*. And this time, it will not just be a soundbite!

So, let us have a closer look at some of the runners and riders – and the arena in which they perform.

This is not going to be pretty.

2 – Avoiding the Rabbit Holes to Split Some Hares

Terminology

For what you are about to receive, may this author make you truly thankful – or not as the case may be. This brief chapter is about terminology, so is therefore bone dry. I have tried to ginger it up but arguably to no avail.

Therefore, if you are comfortable with terms like *agency, recruiter,* and *RPO* – and how they relate to each other (or not) – please feel free to skip over the next few pages. It can nonetheless remain a point of reference.

Those wishing to share my pain should read on.

§

Recruitment is a broad church, albeit with the unholiest of the unholy perched precariously upon its pews. As I have already set the scene, though, our focus will however be on the activists that touch or impact, candidates. Ordinary people like you and me, who will almost certainly have been on the receiving end of the high jinks that reflect the recruiter modus operandi.

Accordingly, I refer throughout the text to *agencies* and *RPOs*. To *recruiters*, who may work in agencies or possibly in-house directly for their own organisations. Some of the tricks of the trade are effortlessly employed by those in whatever recruitment context, while others are specific to a particular sphere of activity. For that reason, I have examined themes rather than industry segments, for want of a better expression. The exception to this was a brief section on '*Volume RPO*'. Its unique context sets it aside for several reasons that will become evident.

There are of course no really clear lines of delineation with recruitment, which is not unique in business. Technically, everything that is not *in-house* could fall within a larger *RPO* umbrella.

§

Recruitment Process Outsourcing (RPO) is when an organisation shifts all or part of its permanent recruitment to an external supplier. RPOs can furthermore act as an extension of an organisation's internal HR function. While not only acquiring staff, they can also introduce technology and methodology to maximise efficiencies, effectiveness, and candidate experience. This can also encompass managing advertising functions. For any one organisation, the RPO could be undertaking one, more, or even all of these activities.

Compared with *contingent agencies* who take a brief to source candidates and who are paid by results, this covers a lot of ground. It is also clear that the remit of agencies could also fall under the notion of outsourced processes and that RPO organisations might be classed as *agencies*. Indeed, sometimes they are. On the question of *volume recruitment*, you might argue that any functioning campaign constituted *volume* per se.

§

As a consequence of the potential confusion hanging over this, I have had to draw the line somewhere and create some working assumptions. Having said that, this should not affect the meaning of what I say because I am largely working with themes.

When I am especially talking about *RPO*, I mean activities that are NOT purely *search and source*. Other references to *recruiter* or *recruiting organisation* pertain to generic activities or practices that are performed pretty much anywhere.

When I talk about *volume recruitment*, I am referring to activities where there are multiple vacancies for the same role, which in practice necessitate bulk processing. The sort of work administered by a contact centre rather than a consultant in an agency office.

The context should make all this clear, but as I have said, it is in any event not going to detract from the points that are going to be made.

Ultimately though, this is all about the candidates.

Which, in the field of recruitment, is a first.

3 – Blessed Are the Kingmakers

The wonderful world of recruiters at work

I will start with the words of the author Leo Rosten who was reputed to have said:

> *'First-rate people hire first-rate people; second-rate people hire third-rate people'.*

Remember those words in the collective mind as a point of reference. How they sum up the organisations in which I have had insight as an employee, client, and supplier...

But for now, on to the matters at hand.

Recruiters...who are they, and what do they do?

An interesting question because they all come in different shapes and sizes. Unlike *Directors*, who come in flavours. Not to mention indiscriminately in some cases. But I digress – and at the earliest juncture ever.

With a blank piece of paper, we would imagine such a person as a *headhunter*. Someone who can spot talent or potential talent and who can see them performing to a high standard in a role that they know intimately well. A psychological jigsaw artist, looking for the perfect piece that will complete their unfinished puzzle. Like spooks gliding through the shadows of Cambridge corridors, seeking out the next Kim Philby. Hmmm, possibly not a great example, but you get the picture.

So, to jot down some notes. *Experts in the chosen field, acutely perceptive, with superb judgement.* Likely to have a high level of authority or at least a high level of trust invested in their abilities by those who do. People on whom the organisation relies in order to keep the ranks swelled with the best talent.

Sound like the people you know in recruitment roles? No, I didn't think so.

That is because that's not the real world, or certainly not the real world in mainstream organisations. Firstly, commercial businesses that have experts do not utilise them to identify and bring in new talent. Experts in organisations are too busy applying their expertise in the furtherance of profit and competitive advantage and that kind of caper. Secondly, experts do not always have sound judgement, which is why they often remain in technical roles rather than moving up the proverbial greasy pole into the world of executive decision-making. Thirdly, in the modern business paradigm, the dynamics of the first-line stages of recruitment are increasingly left to the power of technology to stimulate an initial interest, which can then be assessed and filtered by those in what we now understand to be recruiter roles.

Now that makes a lot of sense. There is a lot of ground to cover in both a volume and geographical sense, so the bait has to be set, and the net has to be cast further afield and cost-effectively in order to get candidates to self-identify. The recruiter's role is then to review what gets captured and to discern, from this, the leads worth pursuing.

So, you see, recruiting is far from being an intelligence-led activity, executed by subject-matter experts with a wider range of psychological and executive skills. That wouldn't stack up for a major blue-chip company.

Of course, that is how it is portrayed and how you are led to believe it all rolls out. More on that later.

It is in fact a volume-based game, driven by numbers, with decisions taken on the basis of sets of rules that have been established beforehand.

Let me first say a few words about the type of *recruiter* you might encounter. Most are *contingent recruiters* – these get paid by results, namely when a successful hire is made. No hire, no fee, so absolutely under pressure to work efficiently. For these, think *High Street Recruiter*, for example.

Recruiters may undertake searches for candidates, who are either active (already seeking opportunities) or passive (not really looking at present). They perform in-depth searches of websites, using *X-ray* techniques to see web content beneath the surface of published pages, Boolean search strings on search engines and the like (you know, searching for 'x AND y NOT z') and networking sites like *LinkedIn*. Some who do not get paid on hire results may be engaged to bolster existing pipelines or get to a credible shortlist. These are *sourcers* rather than pure *recruiters* and those using their services could look at the cost incurred as an alternative to advertisements but with the aim of getting the same (or a better) body of candidates to a fixed stage in the process. The cost will be more expensive depending on the engagement required with candidates, usually higher the more senior the role. The activity selected may range from the *signposting* of a role (sending out a link to apply) to the development of ongoing and more in-depth considerations of the role in partnership.

The sourcing approach reflects more the internal recruiter who is mindful of brand experience and therefore has a greater stake in ensuring that the job is performed more thoroughly, and service is delivered to a higher standard. Occasionally, outsourced providers offer this service, but organisations are rightfully weary of the operators who will take high-end fees for recruiter time and then divert blame onto the latter stages of the process (delivered by the hiring organisation) when final conversion levels are low.

As a candidate, of course you will not easily ascertain exactly how the land lies, but as a golden rule you can be eminently more comfortable if your recruitment contact is *in-house*. Quite simply, they will be more engaged and personally devoted to ethics and service at the very least.

But back to the core considerations at hand.

§

The first thing that recruiters will do on receipt of a request to hire will be to have a look in their CV database to see who might fit the bill, based on what they know. At this stage, they might even put the feelers out and collect updated CVs. You never know, they could immediately strike gold, and this will cut out a lot of legwork on the way to a placement and a fee.

A quick word about recruiters latching onto you. Once you send your CV over, you are *theirs*. They will lay claim to your candidacy for that role, and you are tied to them. Now this can present a problem for you down the line. You see, the recruiter will seek to make contact early on with any possible person who might fit the bill in their databases or through other channels they have out in the market. While they give you the impression that the hiring organisation wants to move quickly, hinting at the 'exclusivity' the hirer has given them, the likelihood is that the hiring organisation will also push out their own advertisement.

Recruiters love the idea of an exclusive arrangement with businesses mainly because – for a limited period at least – they get an open field without competition. For the businesses, they will sometimes allow it if they are naive enough to believe that they will get the recruiter's undivided attention.

As Mr T would say, *'I pity the fools'.*

You see, recruiters shaft their clients with a sense of joy. Do not let their patter tell you otherwise. It is all about the money, honey.

§

Now, over to the hiring organisation and in so far as your candidacy is concerned.

Faced with having to pay an agency a commission of up to 30% of the gross salary for the role, or just falling back on their own pipeline, have a guess which way the wind is going to blow? You guessed right – not in your direction.

So do not get immediately drawn into arrangements with agencies – glean as much information as possible about the role, its location etc and do not commit. Then see what floats to the surface from the business themselves.

If you can then wing over a direct application, you will be in contention on the *right* list or at least the *favoured one* if you are on a par with other great candidates. Whatever you may think, they will save a few grand by appointing a cheaper candidate if they can. It is nearly always about getting, somebody who is good enough. Sometimes, you can be too good, so a greater risk of attrition in the near future.

Do not worry about all the bollocks from agencies saying that they can sell you into the hiring organisation. They only really get to the table with the hard-to-fill roles, or where the client opts to buy from their database rather than biting the bullet on a potentially larger splurge on online media. Even if using an agency, they would likely still advertise online at least through one channel in order to not keep all their hiring eggs in one bastard, sorry, *basket*. Make sure you keep your – and their – options open.

More often than not, they will also quickly post it on an online job board (unless of course the incumbent is still in post and does not know that their sacking is imminent!). You know the popular ones – *TotalJobs*, *Indeed* et al.

It is about generating as much volume as possible that they can sift through to make a shortlist, and at the same time allocate the other CVs to their databases for future reference for other jobs. An early piece of double-bubbling, and why not?

Some of the dastardlier clever chaps will post the job with *The Department of Work and Pensions* (*DWP*), which aggregating job boards *scrape* and list on their sites for free. This is what recruiters refer to as *organic advertising*. *Aggregators* load up their sites with advertisements for free and then, when applicants apply to organisations, the sales staff *prove the concept* of their site and sell promoted advertisements at the same location. As the age-old (but still new) saying goes in the digital world, if you haven't paid for it, *you are the product*.

Anyway, back to our recruiters with their now hefty pile of CVs or applications, and to the next stage in the process, *the sift*.

This sifting will be done in accordance with essential and desirable attributes for the role. These are the parameters set by the hiring manager and bring forth the first challenge.

Yes, incredibly (to outsiders), the hiring manager may not have a thorough understanding of the job themselves. Or they may be working from a *job description* worked up by some flaccid HR Officer, which was inaccurate at inception and has become steadily more inappropriate as time has passed.

This is then shoe-horned into an advertisement template (it is how the self-help bent of online works in practice) where material may be edited out in order to comply with word limits. At this stage, more can be lost in translation because edits are made by those who do not comprehend the import of what they are removing.

Already, it is clear how the whole she-bang can start going awry. The great thing about recruitment exercises is that ten wheels can fall off a four-wheeled cart. It is a joy to behold. Indeed, as long as you are not one of the candidates getting inadvertently shafted.

This all leads to a whole host of people applying who are not suitable, not to mention some good candidates who give it a miss.

Mr Recruiter then filters through the corpus of candidates and makes his shortlist.

Hardly scientific and potentially many steps away from the actual requirement of the organisation. It really is that bad.

Cue John Lennon harmoniously warbling 'HELP!', and with a gaping hole opening up, the recruiter keeps digging.

§

From here, they contact their preferred candidates and work with them to brief them on the role and what to expect. At the same time, they will work with the candidates to refine their CVs to fit the role. This will be the precursor to getting the candidates to interview and helping them to get their best foot forward.

Meanwhile, they will be selling your best attributes to the hiring manager in an attempt to get them in the most receptive frame of mind at the point of interview. Simultaneously, they will be making the candidate feel that they are exclusively on point to be hired (never of course mentioning that you are no more prominent than anyone else on the list of 5 that they have submitted, nor that several other agencies are also putting their own lists forward).

The odds are never quite as good as you are led to believe and, given the disjoints that will already have become embedded in the process up to that point, you may already have been shafted.

At this stage, if you have any queries, the recruiter will pick up your call on the first ring. At that point in the process, your arse is gold.

Now, let us have a closer look and avail ourselves of what the process will likely entail in practice when the recruiter is engaged, reaches out to possible candidates, and posts a job:

- The person heading up the process is an expert on neither the industry nor the hiring organisation. They do not always receive a clear requirement and make a handful of calls to people whom they know will fit the bill.

- They take a brief from an HR bod who themselves is relying on documentation that may or may not reflect the actual requirement, received from a hiring manager who themselves may not know what they actually need.

- The recruiter then takes this and, with their limited knowledge, makes executive decisions on what to include or take out of an advertisement and bangs it out there.

- That same recruiter then applies the rules to an assessment of the CVs to decide who goes through.

- At this stage, the recruiter will have to understand the variety of roles undertaken by candidates in their varying careers in order to fully appreciate whether the candidates meet the requirements. This variability in the body of CVs is huge at this stage even for a pile of, say, 25 CVs.

- The recruiter then needs to be clear on what format and content will be receptive to the hiring manager because they work with you to shape it.

All these steps represent stages of removal from the initial requirement that your application will be at by the time it lands on the hiring manager's desk.

And you feel disheartened when unsuccessful for a job. That it reflects failure on your part?

And when you do fail or are waiting for an update and the hiring manager has not given any prompt initial feedback, you can bet your life that your buttski will no longer be gold in the eyes of the recruiter. *Ghosted* before you can say 'Casper'.

All because you have not been looked after and serviced by an expert. You have been another number in a straightforward numbers game.

At each stage, it has been about shaving down larger numbers to smaller ones and pushing up the probability that the ones that are left will be good enough.

At this point, your expertise means nothing. It may be completely missed at the earlier stages leading to your rejection, or you will simply be part of the pack, with what should be a distinguishing skill not working for you at all.

The recruiter is simply a shit-kicking administrator with limited time who satisfices on numbers and puts clients in a position where, under pressure of time to fill a vacancy – and faced with the choice between mediocre and nothing – will choose mediocre. Every time.

So, we are not talking experts here. Look on *LinkedIn* and see who sits in *Recruitment Consultant* roles. Graduates fresh out of the box in their first job. People who can read and write but are not experts by any stretch of the imagination. Not even experts in *Media Studies* or *Anthropology*, or whatever else they will have studied.

These are sales roles, in the mould of a challenge on *The Apprentice*. They are tossed over something to sell and making the sale is the be-all-and-end all. It is not about making dreams come true for you or even making you happy. It is about commission squeezed out of limited available time.

Recruiters sniff out any dissatisfaction you might have with your current role, and they will be selling their role – and their soul – without a shred of compassion.

If you end up considering a bail-out of a passable job for one that is a pile of turd that they have been unable to fill for several months, do not expect these wankers to flag this up to you. If they even realised it anyway. Once the deal is done, you will have value, only if they think they can place you again, or if you rise to the position where you can help them create more opportunities.

You are probably now starting to form the opinion that High Street recruiters are not the most reputable chaps on the block. Entry-level dullards in the collapsible car to Clownsville. As a candidate, you are nothing but an asset that will outlive its usefulness once either the placement is made, or the hiring manager has gone cold. Unless the wider context changes and they can run you through a different wringer.

§

Not only are the recruiters charged with getting their placements, but they are also additionally burdened with lead generation and building contact networks to help create opportunities. And that, my friend, means cold calling – and lots of it.

Hello, I'd like to speak to Fred Bloggs, please.

Who?

Fred Bloggs – the Head of Operations.

No, John Smith is the Head of Operations.

Oh, sorry, could you please put me through to John?

No, we cannot connect unsolicited calls.

Oh ok. (updates database to reflect that John Smith is the *Head of Operations* and emails him, using what he already knows is the organisation's email address format).

Make no mistake, this is an entry-level cut-throat role that is scientific, only in the sense that eventually some of the shit will stick and a sale will be made.

§

The other gem is in the harvesting of CVs through non-specific job advertisements.

Company confidential, large salary range – or no salary at all, a comment that if you do not hear back after x weeks, assume you have been unsuccessful etc.

All indicators of minimum commitment in exchange for maximum (of your) data.

Spot these and the chances are that you are being harvested. Of course, there are recruiters who are so shit that they really do not update candidates who have been, ahem, rejected. I mean, how difficult must it be to copy and paste an email address into a list and then blind copy out a standard email to all rejected candidates? Granted it is not a great personalised experience, but at least it is *something*.

Most of those shitehawks cannot even be bothered to do that.

But here is one for any hiring organisation to consider, and it is some free consultancy (you are welcome). You are probably familiar with the big *High Street agency* players and may well have been contacting some of the newer, smaller agencies. The boutique, niche players. You know, the ones with funky names like *Green Worm*, or where the founder has taken the Christian names of his two children as the name of his business, which also helps to keep alive the faintest embers of his loveless marriage. These agencies are however the biggest clowns in the circus. The ones who spend the first 10-15 years of their career with one of the big players (check them out on *LinkedIn*) and then leave to set up their agency overnight.

How do they manage that? Wow, is it because they are fearless, maverick entrepreneurs? I really do not know. Quick, round to 221B Baker Street to get Sherlock on the case.

Ok, I will tell you – *they stole client lists and contacts and approached them on the sly before they resigned*.

And if they can do that to the people who have nurtured and helped them and given them their break (naturally the High Street agencies are absolute wankers themselves, so no great sympathy there), what do you think they are going to do to you? And how will they treat their candidates?

Answers on a postcard, please. The bottom line is that it will not benefit anyone other than these morally corrupt reprobates themselves.

§

So back to our harvesters.

Applications come in and they get themselves a whole host of relevant CVs for the database for when a real requirement comes in. Then they bulk-email out the new opportunity, at the same time that the job is posted on a board. Minimal effort, maximum funnel (I will go into that in more detail later).

When you chase for updates on these jobs, you get the inevitable fob-offs about delays even to the point where some of these recruiters claim that the client/hiring manager has ghosted *them*. They have got the backbone of an eel, these slippery fish. Flipping it so that they are the victims. You couldn't make it up.

You have to ask yourself what kind of commercial relationship recruiters have with businesses. Well, the answer is that these relationships are not the greatest. By and large, organisations loathe recruitment agencies. And when I say loathe, I mean *loathe*.

People are not stupid. They know that recruiters are lazy, incompetent, and immoral. And these are just the more ethical ones. But what they do is deal with the crap that nobody else has time for and they do go for gratuitous hospitality several times a year. Therefore, for hiring managers in organisations, it is about as much free booze as you can chisel out of them in exchange for business that somebody somewhere is going to have to pick up. There is also certainly the fact that today's clients become tomorrow's candidates, so a little mutual backscratching may also not go amiss.

As a candidate though, you need to take a step back and avoid the full-on emotional commitment to these *opportunities*. Like allowing your mind to strongly visualise yourself in-post, or even mentally re-organising finances and future life plans. With an intermediary in play – particularly a tossbox recruiter – your grip on the actual status of your application will be a loose one. Sometimes you will be practically dead in the water, and you will still be strung along on the off chance that they can wheedle you back into contention. Just try and avoid the personal pitfalls that can send you into a spiral, at least until you have met the hiring manager and can afford the matter some personal judgement.

Yes, a good job helps with self-esteem. But not getting one, does not make you a failure.

This isn't about a professionally run process, with any consistent rules, where talent and ability shine through and are fairly rewarded. It is a warped game played by warped people for money.

And they will place whoever fits the bill in accordance with the way that circumstances converge.

You just need to understand the mechanisms and play them, without getting too emotionally attached. Then if you do not succeed on occasions, it is at best because the odds were stacked against you by the cumulative variables that I have outlined, or at worst because you didn't play the game well enough.

And that – from a self-esteem perspective – really shouldn't trouble you too much.

4 – Brigands, Not Talent!

The growth and expansion of 'Talent Management' functions

What I do love about organisational life in general is that concepts hurtle about and are appropriated by people and incorporated into daily activities, and nobody really has a Scooby-Doo what they mean. Or more pertinently, what they should be doing in order to cover the detail that will fulfil the promise of whatever concept that might be.

None is more splendid than the notion of *Talent Management*, alongside the more traditional concepts of *Recruitment* and *Resourcing*.

Now we can attempt to define all these terms, but in many respects, they overlap and there are no clear and discrete categorisations. In common parlance, *Recruitment* is the process of searching for prospective employees and generating interest so that they will make applications. So really, Recruitment is about discovering sources and connecting with them so that they apply.

However, the notion of Recruitment for many organisations extends into processes for selection, right up to, and sometimes slightly beyond, the decision to hire. Therefore, a *Recruitment Manager* might oversee an end-to-end process from the point that a job is advertised to the moment that a candidate is offered a job, or even during the onboarding process between job offer, acceptance and day one in-post.

The term *Resourcing* is more about understanding the longer-term needs of an organisation and ensuring that people with appropriate talents are in place. Nevertheless, you may sometimes have resourcing professionals overseeing parts of recruitment processes. But really, *Resourcing Managers* should always have a very close ongoing relationship with hiring managers, so they can stay one step ahead of the curve and ensure that vacancies do not remain unfilled for long. Perhaps even achieving the Holy Grail of filling a position before the end of a notice period and having *a handover*. Well, if you get that, something somewhere is working fine.

So back in the room and the real world.

§

When it comes to making an application for a job, you may be interacting with people in the *Resourcing Team* or the *Recruitment Team*. What is now increasingly more likely, is that you may encounter so-called *Talent Management* specialists. The reason for this is that organisations have recognised that hand-offs from hiring managers to recruitment teams and vice versa lead to strategic gaps appearing in their businesses. People drop the ball, or perhaps more relevantly, others fail to pick it up. The introduction of *Talent Management* as a concept allows for a greater degree of joined-up thinking so that vacancies and gaps are anticipated and that there is a clearer view of capability existing within an organisation, that a purely outwardly facing *Recruitment* function might not have within their remit. I suppose in many senses, this appreciation of internal talent used to fall within the gift of the *Personnel Manager*. Before the creation of *HR* that is. And what a resounding success that was! Not.

Unfortunately, just in the way that some aspects of *Resourcing* have become sucked into the scope of a *Recruitment Team*, there has also been a considerable amount of inconsistency in the way that so-called *Talent Management* experts work in practice. Frequently, *Talent Specialists* perform purely *Resourcing* or purely *Recruitment* roles. Or they may see the priority of someone concerned with *'Talent'* as being that of *attraction* or *acquisition*. Presumably, somebody who has the job title of *Talent Acquisition Specialist* is indeed simply a recruiter at the very first stage of a process to identify and secure the interest of a potential candidate.

Now the importance of all of this for you as a candidate is to prevent you from taking at face value what any of these individuals might be doing, should you come into contact with them. If you meet a *Recruitment Consultant*, you just need to understand that these people are concerned with getting you into the top of the process. These are the bods who waft out the sizzle but who have no interest in providing you with a quality steak.

Resourcing Specialists are those who work with hiring managers to identify organisational needs and who make sure that the *Recruitment* activity is on track to deliver those objectives. While Recruiters sometimes deal with *Resourcing* matters, it would be exceedingly rare for a candidate to deal directly with a *Resourcer* before being hired. If as a candidate, you find you are dealing directly with a member of the *Resourcing* team, this should set alarm bells ringing about the type of job you are being lined up for. This is because *Resourcers* are ones with immediate needs to resolve, so the likelihood is the role you are probing is a quick-hire and possibly quick-fire grunt job, more suited for an agency temp.

Think about who were the people in your former companies who would deal with temping agencies, i.e. (external) *Recruiters*. They will absolutely have been members of the *Resourcing* team. Therefore, as a direct candidate, you should be really concerned if members of the Resourcing team are reaching out to you. They are likely going to be going *Route 1* for *bums on seats* rather than incurring the expense of engaging an agency. Remember that employers can now dismiss employees with less than 2 years' service, without fear of an unfair dismissal claim (as long as discrimination is not involved). Many are relying on this to take on direct hires and avoid agency costs. Beware people. Unless of course, you are happy with that kind of role that would more likely be suitable for those seeking temporary agency positions.

§

This brings me to those with *Talent Management* or *Talent Specialist* in their job titles. These will likely be people who have been given a very far-ranging brief to undertake within the organisation. While at the same time as being interested in the attraction of suitable candidates and the recruitment process, they should also be undertaking resourcing-related activities. Seeking to understand not only external recruitment requirements but also internal moves. These are the ones who should be building very strong relationships with hiring managers in order to understand the likelihood of internal movements.

Therefore, their attention should be focused on driving internal debate and planning with regard to existing talent so that when difficult-to-fill vacancies arise the company can reset the internal balance of talent. As a result, replacements are not simply a quest for like-for-like swaps. Let me explain.

Let us consider a situation where an incumbent has been in a role for 5 years. When they were initially hired, this was done in accordance with a job description. Over the 5 years of service in-role, that individual will likely have taken on additional responsibilities, looking after work that previously fell into other areas but needed to be assumed for reasons of operational efficacy e.g. when other changes took place. People will frequently pick up new responsibilities, depending on the skills they themselves develop, or if others are working on projects, and tasks need to be reallocated. This is generally accepted and indeed, an objective, in order to further personal development.

Moreover, in time, the remit of any individual will in any event develop organically. Now, at a point where an individual then leaves the organisation, the gap that needs to be filled is often larger and of a different shape than that denoted by the job description alone. This then presents a particular challenge for anybody in recruitment because the role has in effect 'grown arms and legs'. Getting a like-for-like replacement is going to be much more of a challenge. This is because, in Boolean terms, as your search string becomes more complex, your available pool becomes a lot smaller.

Search for *'football player'* online and you will get a large pool of results. Search for *'football player Real Madrid 100 caps'*, and the number of results returned will be considerably smaller. The role of the *Talent Specialist* within an organisation should be to anticipate these changes or at least be aware of how work can be reallocated so that the *Recruitment Team* can search for a more generalised skill set when a vacancy arises. The end result is that you still have the right number of people within the organisation to do the work that needs to be completed. You are not simply continuing to organise your workforce in exactly the same way following the resignation of one or more employees. If you try to do this, you are in effect advertising for *unicorn candidates*.

But make no mistake, that is what countless moronic enterprises foist upon the job-seeking public. Updated job descriptions and person specifications, for which only one excellent candidate exists. *The one who has just left*.

Therefore, as a candidate, if you see a lengthy job description with a tremendously detailed range of responsibilities for the role, the chances are that there is no effective *strategic talent management* in place within the organisation. And if you make contact with the company to discuss the role in more detail and the person who speaks to you identifies themselves as a *Talent Management Specialist* or the like, you can be absolutely sure that such a person is shit at their job.

Either way, you will have an uphill task in getting hired, or if you are hired, you are going to be set up to fail in a company that has not appreciated the dynamic and evolving nature of talent. If you have not already grasped this underlying theme, the concept of *talent* is very much an overworked and fatigued concept in the recruitment industry. The sense is that if you should use the *talent* label on anything you wish to pump up or bolster, no matter how little substance it has.

'Hire good candidates' or *'win the War for Talent'?* Take a guess what is going to win the day...

The marriage between *talent* and the recruitment industry could be symbolised alternatively as *talent confetti*. It is thrown about indiscriminately and left to the conscientious among us to clear up. The so-called *War for Talent* is for the most part the *war for volume*. The supposed *Talent Specialists* are for the most part *Recruitment Officers*. Any organisation with a high-profile *Talent Management Team* will betray their lack of competence if their job advertisements are overly complex.

So, on a practical level, I am not asking you to be too judgemental whether you speak to a *Recruiter* or a *Talent Acquisition Specialist*. But I am saying, if you are dealing directly with *Resourcing*, be very careful. I am also stating that if there is a big play made of *Talent Management* or *Talent Specialists*, take a really close look at the bigger picture and the wider context. It may be the difference between stepping into a minefield or, in the best traditions of the *News of the World*, making your excuses and leaving.

As an aside, do not trouble yourself with any efforts to decipher the *Resourcing Business Partner* or *Talent Business Partner* job titles. These are simply vacuous titles dreamt up by unscrupulous and delusional imposter businesses to convince stakeholders that *Recruiters* and *Resourcers* are closely aligned to organisational objectives. Make no mistake, they rarely will be, and as a candidate, they will not enter your world. If you do spot these, make a mental note that the business concerned is trying just a tad too hard to emphasise the obvious work that recruitment and resourcing teams should be undertaking anyway.

As one final comment, I have made a number of references to the *Recruitment 'industry'*. However, as you will doubtless discover, you can scarcely imagine a less industrious crew of charlatans. And as my background is in BPO contact centres, when it comes to spotting disreputable shysters, I am something of a connoisseur.

It will not be possible to always spot them all, or if you can, as early as you would like. This game is all about being on high alert and minimising the probability of getting stung.

On with the journey and to the almost unfathomable longevity of the *Curriculum Vitae* – or *CV*.

5 – Your History...

The incredible staying power of the curriculum vitae

Life always throws up those pleasant and endearing snippets of happiness and yesterday I saw on television that some guy is still religiously playing VHS tapes. Yes, watching *Rambo* and *Desperately Seeking Susan* and the like, with all their momentarily distorted sound, merging colours and flickering. Like vinyl enthusiasts, I am sure that he feels a certain amount of affinity to the nostalgic context as he goes back through his old films. Not just watching the films but *remembering what it was like when he first watched them*. Which all got me thinking about CVs.

Why are people still using them at all? And how is it that they have grown arms and legs? It is almost off the scale of ultra-bonkers for an activity that purports to follow process, objectivity, and legislation.

I mean, in the UK and Commonwealth countries, a CV contains only a summary of employment history, qualifications, education, and some personal information. A brief document of introduction, so to speak. Essentially, this is what some now call a resumé, or at least they do in countries where a CV is more an in-depth and detailed summary of academic and medical achievements, incorporating publications and wider elements.

But in UK employment circles, the CV has now necessitated the degree of content of the above and is used as a sifting tool. Essentially, a recruiter will very likely review your CV and decide whether or not you will progress.

Sounds a little problematic? Well to the discerning and rounded individual, yes. To a *recruiter*, not on your life. I cannot think of a *High St recruiter* who would not bounce you in or out of contention on a cursory read of your CV. It is hugely contradictory within the context of objective recruitment but rarely even questioned. Let us look at the context a little more closely:

- Firstly, there is no standard format, so for a jobseeker it is impossible to gauge what should be in or out. You have to second-guess the preferences of the hiring manager.

- Or second-guess the recruiter and hope that the hiring manager shares the same perspective with them. This always brings forth a degree of subjective guff from the twats who get that piece of interpretation wrong.

- Then, you have to be bank on the fact that the recruiter or hiring manager (or both) understands your CV. Do not assume that they will fully appreciate the nature of your roles undertaken or the relevance of your qualifications.

If you are unfortunate on any of these, or worse still, on a combination of any of these factors, you may well find your application winging its way into oblivion. Yes, that place where it is forgotten, forever.

And you will likely not even get a notification to tell you why.

So, some like them detailed and some set a maximum of two pages. Some say detail all the achievements and notable results.

Others like you to tailor the CV to suit the role (hmm, can be interesting if the job description is off the mark as previously discussed), others say keep the CV straightforward and factual, with a bespoke cover letter highlighting your relevance for the role.

Everybody's got an opinion, but you see the challenge. And once again, your application is at the mercy of someone else. And that's before the merits of your track record have been considered at all.

So, if I am advised to limit the length of my CV and the recruiter has misunderstood the role, or the job description is inaccurate, I might delete relevant achievements from my tailored CV.

Yes, that happens very frequently in fact. And then you will be dropkicked through the posts, without ever knowing why. You will probably already have worked out that in these cases, the recruiter will not be jumping forward at any time soon with feedback that exposes their own ineptitude.

§

One popular theme from the critics concerns the lack of standardisation of CVs, so this does raise question-marks on fairness and the ability to objectively compare candidates. Yes, with the job-seeking public, absolutely. A cause for concern among recruiters though? Is it heck? And who do you think you are to question all their years in recruitment? Well, that's their argument anyway.

Of course, they do have a point. They are hired to sift, and their judgement is trusted without question. And as any legal beagle will tell you, tribunals do not challenge recruitment decisions per se – only those where a protected characteristic either directly or indirectly can be evidenced to have driven the decision. Picking somebody incompetent or unqualified through a hasty sift is seen as a cross for the organisation to bear and likely a lucky escape for the unsuccessful candidate.

In other words, tough titties.

Some organisations, to their credit, have attempted to use structured application forms with CV-relevant sections so that any information collected is comparable and less susceptible to creative manipulation. But even this is flawed if candidates are swiftly removed on a CV-type review in the first instance.

After all, if there are minimum eligibility questions, these can easily be asked from the off, and exclusion on this basis can be comfortably justified. But a CV sift that looks at achievements and experience? The better sift processes will be more structured, with points earned for specific criteria, but a lot will still rest on subjective assessment, the capability of the sifter, and on occasion plain luck.

For the dissenters, all is not completely lost because there is a strong argument for an unfair process if it is not stated in advance that a CV sift will take place against key criteria. In those cases, it is probably a must to tailor the CV for the role, no matter how intuitively wrong that might seem. Again, it is all about playing the game.

§

The problem for the voices of reason in getting themselves heard is that nobody has to listen. And take it from me that very few will be listening. You will be odds-on whistling in the wind when you question the exalted position of the CV.

And it is not just the unreliability and inconsistency of the documentation and how that is put together.

The process for reviewing them will often be equally wild.

In most cases, the CV sift will be unstructured. There will not be a huge amount of time to dedicate to each CV (probably one to two minutes), so it will be less about the depth of achievement and qualification and more about catching their eye.

Think about it. Fifty CVs alone, fifteen minutes to read and digest each one and make some notes? Would be a push to get one done in fifteen minutes anyway. That's more than one and a half working days solid and to achieve what? To get down to fifteen CVs perhaps. I see the argument that it is time well spent in order to get down to the best fifteen.

Recruiter*s* do not see it that way. They just want 15 who look ok. Job done in minimal time.

Enough to make you weep really, that any organisation would risk either progressing a moron or losing a great candidate on such a whim.

So, take a few minutes to look around you and compute how many morons got hired in your own office and whether you can feel a paucity of real talent?

When I did it, it resonated massively. Thank you, Leo Rosten.

For a moment though, let us hark back to the *getting the best talent* argument of the recruiters. Not only have we shown that this is a fundamentally flawed argument from the off – at the attraction stage – it is now starkly obvious that even if (some of) the best talent is caught in the initial net, it can very easily fall away for purely unmeritorious reasons.

You will start to recognise a common theme about these 'processes'. The more they progress, the more random and more distant from science and fairness they become.

Unfortunately, to compound your already-escalating sense of disappointment at these processes, CV sifters are the greatest (and I use that term quantitatively) exponents of *halo and horns*. If you *feel* like a previously good employee that they know, that will greatly increase your chances of falling into the *'yes' pot*. If you have unfortunate similarities to a *wrong'un*, you may be closer to the bin. That can even, and unfortunately, especially be driven by the fact that you share a previous workplace with someone they already know.

Discrimination is also rife, based on race, religion and university attended.

Even if you switch off any conscious bias, the unconscious leanings we all have will come to the fore in some shape or form. The idea that CVs can form any part of a selection process, other than background information for interviews (once suitably redacted) is premier league stupidity, but recruiters are wedded to CV sifting like Catholics are to Mass. It is ingrained in them. Whatever objective and psychometrically driven process you put their way; they will be looking for a CV.

I have seen candidates pass through expertly designed processes, designed by chartered organisational psychologists, and earn the right to an interview in accordance with an agreed process. Only then to fail to secure an interview because some recruitment droid wanted to see their CV before confirming.

Recruiters and hiring managers cannot resist measuring candidates against their own infallible judgement. Which, more often than not, is completely shot away and driven by their own egotistical and erroneous self-assessment. If they were *that* good at spotting talent, they would recognise that they were themselves crap.

The problem is that the majority of managers are so absurdly self-unaware, with their heads permanently lodged either in a spreadsheet or up a senior arsehole. Recruiters are so entrenched in their cliched spiels that they have a very tenuous grip on what is going on in the real world.

§

Finally, you may come across the highly dubious and unscrupulous shysters who will offer you a free review of your CV. You will then get a (templated) report highlighting what needs to be changed, followed by a quote to re-write it and your inbox mercilessly strafed by follow-up emails to push you to part with your hard-earned fold.

For all the reasons I have outlined, please do not fall for this fictional nonsense. How can anybody design you a great CV, when they have absolutely no knowledge of the preferences of who is going to read it or the criteria used by those who might be scoring it?

Their sales pitch is premised on a wholesome fallacy. They are selling a one-size-fits-all product, when we all know that real-world situations are defined by the variability of features and circumstances.

Do not let them suck you in.

If you have experiences or knockbacks, the likelihood is that your CV will fail due to the crazy and unmeasured processes applied to its review. I have seen grim-looking CVs sail straight through because it was evident that the candidate was well-qualified with a depth and breadth of experience.

Not because of calligraphy, formatting, and lavender parchment.

And as we are about to discover, the roles that are being targeted may not even be real...

6 – On a Role

When is a role, not a role?

Charlatans, by their nature, gloss over detail and encourage those around them to be carried away by their assumptive manner. To *believe* and to *accept*. Now this is all fine, but evidence needs to precede any conclusions on anything.

The only way to counter this is to always start at the beginning and ask some seemingly obvious questions. Never be embarrassed by this. It is the fear of such embarrassment that allows the flimflammers to thrive.

You also need to ask questions about common factors in debates that everybody, not just the rogues, takes for granted. It is in these areas that the unscrupulous will prosper unchallenged.

So here we go.

We know that recruiters identify suitable people for roles, but what makes a role a role? You may feel that such a question is pointless, but believe me, nothing is straightforward in this game.

To answer this, we need to take a momentary step back to appreciate how a role becomes defined. In basic terms, a *Head of Department* or function will look at the outputs they need to create at any given time and will draw up the structure chart of the various specialists or non-specialists that they need to perform the work.

And what do they base this on? Essentially opinions (based on experience) of their own and/or other stakeholders (assuming that the *Head* is not some lunatic despot – but do not rule it out!) and some rudimentary mathematics, where they piece together the units of work that they anticipate will come through and the volume of individual tasks related to the skills needed to produce them.

Already, you can probably see the challenges with this approach.

Uneven distribution of work generally leads to considerable variability in sub-task categories.

Opinions are opinions, often based on experience, that provide no guarantee of future workflows or work content.

Add to this, wider contextual changes – advances in technology, evolving client and supplier circumstances to name but a few – and we have a pretty volatile context within which to make firm commitments about roles.

But that is what organisations do, and they seek to define these very rigidly because there will be HR teams whose professional stance will dictate that ongoing performance management of individuals will be severely problematised if people are unclear on what is expected of them. They think this because everything – owing to their robotised tunnel-vision process fanaticism – has to be bolted down into processes *that they control*. While they love to tell managers that it is not their job to manage staff, they absolutely want to control staff through managers, control managers and control agendas. Lower than the lowest of the low.

Never forget that no matter how chummy, the HR person has no loyalty to you. Only to themselves, which they achieve by selling you out to the business.

But let us revert to the topic at hand before I write the next 20 pages on HR low jinx.

So, in our job design process, we arrive at the next step, where HR professionals define the roles and set them into stone once the hiring manager – based on all this uncertainty – has articulated their needs. At this stage, there may be some *job analysis* performed, whereby people who are already performing work related to the new role, will have this mapped back into identifiable responsibilities.

It is all a complete farce. Why? Because it is all about documenting processes and specifications that look great as standalone documents but are necessarily misaligned with real-life situations and challenges.

What happens in practice is that people are hired and then generally sink or swim. Those who need clarity and structure will very likely sink in the more entrepreneurial or unregulated organisations.

Those who thrive, tend to make the job their own and take in more and more, expanding their remit because they build the knowledge and skills that allow them to do so.

Senior managers, who do like to take the path of least resistance, let this situation roll – it is less hassle to do so, and the job gets done. It also keeps the hungry ones happier, for a while at least.

But it is a big-time strategic error in exchange for short-term results and an easier ride.

When these employees leave, the gap that needs to be filled will either be for a *unicorn candidate* or will necessitate a reshuffle of the pack – often extensively – and the likely increase of headcount by more than the one leaver in question. Or the management team piss off the remaining staff, who have to step out of their comfort zone and from a standing start take on role fragments for which they are ill-suited and in some cases to which they are bitterly opposed.

So, one way of looking at this is that it panders short-term to the people who end up leaving anyway and hacks off the loyal staff who stay while threatening the quality outputs of your business.

Nice work.

§

The other point about all this is that we have become so HR-led and risk-averse that organisations are missing a gargantuan trick. You see, with empowered managers, you can employ staff with very high-level job descriptions and allow line managers to take the lead with them on what is required.

As long as the line management is solid, and performance is reviewed – and documented where necessary – businesses can avoid being hamstrung by rigid job descriptions that are obsolete by the time the *HR Officer* walks over to the printer.

However, businesses do not want managers to be managers. They want them to be the administrators of processes. And your Janus *HR Director* wants to control the whole lot while naturally not assuming any direct responsibility or accountability.

For recruitment, this means that jobs that do not exist are advertised in the vain hope of attracting candidates who do not exist, administered by recruiters who understand neither the jobs, nor the candidates, nor the context.

It is a rum old world.

Then, what happens is that they go through this bullshit volume game, where lines of candidates are sifted in the most cursory and time-efficient manner and then sent through to clients, who at first reject and reject. Then – when time is critically against them – they re-set client expectations and hire the best of the rest.

By this time, the essentials and desirables of the job description are fluttering in the wind. Along with the competitive advantage being sought by the hiring manager and the wider organisation. But for the recruiter, the fee remains the same.

In fact, they can even make more money by performing shite and doing minimal legwork. As long as the client has been whipped up into such desperation, they will accept any old mug.

Welcome to paradise.

7 – The External Hard Drive

Are they going to go 'internal' or 'external'?

Be neither surprised nor disappointed when the *internal candidate* lands the role on which you have not only pinned your hopes but about which you were led to believe you would be an uncontested shoo-in.

Hell, there may have been a great internal candidate waiting in the wings, who was going to excel for their management acumen and who also had unparalleled tacit knowledge. You benchmarked brilliantly but lost out to the fact that an equally stellar manager would have been able to 'hit the ground running'. It does happen. But not so disproportionately for internal appointments that actually get made.

So, what is it about *internals*? And I do not mean the times when your proctologist gets to look up an old friend.

Well first off, they are cheaper. Sometimes as much as 50% cheaper. And in the world of salaries, that's a lot of big.

They are also likely to be institutionalised and this, for your everyday sociopathic departmental manager, borders on the orgasmic. A large slice (possibly even all) of the facts and data inside their little internal pinheads will have been transplanted into them by the hiring company, and frankly they are scared at the prospect of having to leave. As a result, they do not tend to look outside, are desperate to accept any offer and on the off chance they manage to snag an external interview, they will bomb like Jewish Christmas. Which incidentally emasculates them further within their existing organisation.

But you have to look wider than the candidates themselves and think about who the hiring managers are.

In the twenty-first century workplace, we have been witnessing a new industrial revolution – the beginnings of a *Fourth Industrial Revolution*. The *First Industrial Revolution* harnessed water and steam power in order to drive mechanical production. The *Second* adopted electric power to ramp up the scale of outputs to mass production. The *Third* incorporated electronics and information technology into processes to underpin automation. The *Fourth* is the development of digitisation, which is redrawing previously clear geographical, physical, and even biological lines.

As a result, jobs are changing, whole organisations are evolving. Sometimes disappearing.

Some senior managers are seeing a lot of their favourite staples just disappearing as obsolete.

Heads of advertising agencies now find themselves overseeing social media hubs. Housing department chiefs, who used to run whole bureaucratic paper-spaffing monoliths, are now *Customer Access Directors*, overseeing the development of self-help online portals. You even have *Big Data Experts* – who knows who they were 10 years ago?

And many of them do not have the first clue, let alone a remote interest. They are just motivated by the prospect of freewheeling through the final years of employment, buoyed by the additional prospect of releasing some pension funds at fifty-five (thanks Mr Osborne.)

So, these characters are hardly likely to want to bring in any movers and shakers who are going to raise questions about their own obvious incompetence and seemingly ceaseless jiggery-pumpery. Fresh blood who will point out the fact that their new bosses are so far off best practice that they would need one of Richard Branson's intergalactic massage wands to get back to *'disengaged'*.

In some organisations, this might be betrayed implicitly by any new gunslingers revolutionising operations to the extent that somebody asks the pertinent question of *why none of it had been managed before*.

No Sir-ee, they will fall back on the low-maintenance internal candidate, who costs less, has a high level of tacit knowledge and whose bumbling ineptitude as a manager and a leader can be masked under the guise of 'development' or the structure of process and procedure.

Understandably, there is an added consideration to be taken here. Not only will the organisation have lost a worker who needs to be replaced, but they might also risk a further resignation from the prospective internal candidate who feels that the development opportunities that they have doubtless been promised have not materialised. So, the promotion of an internal candidate might often kill two birds or at least potential birds, with one stone.

Hmmm, you can almost feel that prospect stirring the loins of your average blue-suited, tan-winklepickered recruitment superhero.

What further buttresses the position of an incompetent internal candidate is the strategic exchange that takes place between other long-standing colleagues who work in the organisation, particularly those who will now need to report to the incompetent. They could of course leave as the ones with most integrity do. Understandably, there are practical financial considerations in leaving without a job to go to.

So, in exchange for ticking certain boxes that can be stitched together as a succession of positive performance indicators for an outside audience, those experienced hacks will not be pushed outside their comfort zone by their new boss. They in turn will provide support for the way things are run and will not rock the boat.

The result will be that the internal hire mooches along in their role, not stretching any boundaries and not being stretched by their boss who neither understands their role, his role, nor the wider business context. Of course, this is all to the detriment of the business.

Any business challenges, such as the emergence of service failures or dissatisfied customers, will then be met with the line that issues were 'inevitable', foreshadowed by the usual tactic of *'contexting'* as I outlined in *Flypaper for Freaks*. This is where managers will set down fake contexts in advance so that different outcomes can be more easily and more palatably explained to a critical stakeholder.

The issue for the external candidate is that they will be continuing to exert a tremendous amount of effort into the application process, while the hiring decision will often have been taken before the role had even scraped its way onto the first half-page of the organic search engine results.

You can sometimes spot these little internal honeypots with the odd and very specific lines in 'essential requirements' that will be so precise on combinations of essentials that it would be very challenging for an external chap to achieve.

'A technical accountant, ACA-qualified, with 10 years Big 4 PQE, a proven track record of having implemented new systems in Middle Eastern non-profits'.

So, unless you are Abdul from Baghdad, assistant underling in *Accounts Receivable* at the Qatar branch, you will have to be honest with yourself about whether you truly can demonstrate excellence in all these areas. If you cannot and you slip through (particularly with public sector roles where they may have a vested interest in at least interviewing externals to 'prove' the objectivity of the process) it is likely to prove to be a false economy.

Don't waste your time and effort in putting yourself through it. Direct your energies onto something much more rewarding. Like smashing your own face into a brick wall.

It is frustrating to be rejected in these circumstances, but the most important thing for the candidate is to recognise the pitfalls early on in the process so that they can manage their own expectations and also the amount of effort that they will apply to the process. Furthermore, they need to assess whether this is commensurate with the likelihood of success. It is all about not allowing the merry-go-round to whip up a whole host of negative emotions that will synergise and drag you into a downward spiral. Believe me, these recruiters and organisations will not give a second thought to you or your well-being, and in some cases, where you were never at the races, you will just be seen as cannon fodder that legitimises their process.

And they will all just be sitting there in their funky little city-centre office, vacantly twanging their *Every Mind Matters* wristbands.

You have to draw a line under these kinds of situations because you cannot fight corruption where the finer details just aren't accessible. It kills you even more when you know something is bent but that you will never be able to prove it. It is like that feeling when you are falsely accused but cannot clear your name. It hurts way more than the shame of being caught out for something you have actually done.

With the snide internal shoehorn promotions, there's nothing you can do. Ultimately, they can make their hiring decisions with impunity, providing you cannot evidence any discrimination. And digging up evidence of that, well you have a better chance of sourcing some rocking-horse shit.

They may for example disguise their chicanery by pulling jobs, then appointing people to the same job with a different job title, only to gradually assimilate this into the intended structure over time. Invariably the hire will be shite, so there's always a payback of sorts.

You might be lucky though and get a small pay rise if you start to raise complaints, just to keep you quiet. Of course, take the money if it is offered, but learn the lesson. For a few grand, they will forget all the principles of fairness they purport to espouse in their endless floods of piss-poor marketing content. Start making plans to leave because they will have no compunction to shaft you when it is comfortable for them to do so.

None of this can happen without the support of weak, corrupt, and snide *HR Managers* who on the one hand squat down at your desk for their *everyman* chats – you know, if you like Football, they will like Football. You like *Kylie*, they will like *Kylie*. All the time they are collecting snippets, information to knife you and to limit your opportunities and maximise theirs. You will know who they are in your organisation, the shameless and scurrilous rats. The ones who happily slip into elevated roles themselves, without any sense of them having ever been advertised and for which such advertisement would be their own professional and legal responsibility.

Scumbags.

§

Let me avail you of a brief tale of one organisation I know, namely the story of *'Droid'* (not their real name, of course). Now Droid is one of your typical social warrior types, a true centre-left luvvie who spent a number of years, poncing about in dead-end jobs. Apart from a brief stint in a shop, Droid has never worked outside of their current organisation. They bring nothing to the party, aside from unswerving obsequiousness and fanatical loyalty to the top brass.

In the course of but a few years, Droid is popping up in all sorts of different roles but has never been appointed through an objective process. In every job, they display a narrow-minded focus on data, spreadsheets and bureaucracy but deliver nothing tangible of note. In spite of their obvious incompetence, they continue an inexorable rise, unassailable through their thorough integration into an inveterately nepotistic culture.

Droid just spends all day long scouring the Internet for ideas and management concepts that they can hopelessly seek to apply in the wrong context, leaving colleagues in a state of bewilderment, or putting together a seemingly endless string of slides that celebrate, what they are deluded enough to believe is their 'leadership'.

Of course, Droid does not know any different.

Totally and utterly incompetent, yet totally and utterly safe in their role.

Meanwhile, Droid's team are leaving (60% in just over a year) and the ones who remain are those who are happy at being free to coast. After all, Droid does not have the knowledge or drive to push them on to greater achievements. They of course could not care less that Droid is a car crash because they are getting an easy ride.

Now, I would like to report that this is a business that has not quite got to grips with modern organisational development theory and practice. Alas, it is one that purports to fly the flag for securing the best talent and championing objective assessment. Shamelessly there they are, with a high-profile example of everything that contradicts those principles to the core.

Almost inconceivable, but it is happening right now. A place so warped that its 'leaders' feel more comfortable with failure by insiders than with progress and pushing the boundaries from those outside the clique.

While some businesses are cut-throat to the extreme for money, money, money, you had better believe that others see their organisations as a nest to be feathered for the collective clique.

A comfortable boys' club, with more effort spent on getting away with murder than attending to the deliverables of the organisation. The great thing about it (for them) is that if they get rumbled, they simply move on to the next company and start up a new club. Whole careers are fashioned from the delivery of nothing.

Walking out of their weekly meeting, always joking, with their pads under their arms, filled with their notes that they take and never again review. Evidence that turds really do float to the top of the pan.

Paradoxically, Droid is lauded as an example of positive policies towards internal promotion and as an incentive for others to join the organisation. The fact that this business loses clients at an astronomically rapid rate is nothing more than collateral damage. It is painful to watch, but that's how some companies are run.

They only realise they have cataclysmically ballsed up when it is too late though even then go into denial about the reasons why it has all crashed. In fact, in this case, the more people pointed out how crassly inept Droid was, the more the senior managers escalated their commitment to Droid. Even to the point of falsely attributing success stories to Droid's contribution to the business. You can almost imagine the Managing Director sitting there sobbing, like an alcoholic downing meths, knowing that it is killing him.

'Yeh, that'll show them'.

This is not a solitary example, so time for a quick R2 detour. There are similar tales the length and breadth of the country while organisations struggle to get to grips with the concepts of *Recruitment, Resourcing, Talent Acquisition* and *Performance Management*, let alone how they might strategically relate to one another.

It is a strange paradox that the process of recruitment is always positioned as a quest for the very best talent. Yet in practice, while recruiting the best talent is frankly impossible, what people actually want for their organisations is considerably less than even the mediocre. It is all just about keeping collective heads above water at the lowest possible cost.

But as Red Adair was reputed to have said: *'If you think it's expensive to hire a professional, wait until you hire an amateur'.*

8 – Back of the Net!

Fishing for numbers – attracting candidates into the pipelines.

Don't you just love those little categorisations and disciplines that industries conjure up and mould into a pithy term that elevates the mundane to the wonderfully conceptual?

Like *Candidate Attraction*. It makes it sound so personable and agreeable. Much better than *'building pipelines',* or *'getting the numbers in'.*

One of the great things about candidate attraction is that the world has changed so much in the last 20 years. You cannot beat progress, eh? So, methods of attraction that were hugely popular at the turn-of-the-century, scarcely scratch the surface now. I mean, there was a time when candidate attraction was almost predominantly about placing print advertisements in newspapers and magazines. And it was a massively lucrative business for those involved in recruitment advertising.

But now, while print advertisements still do exist, the balance has shifted towards, in the first instance online advertising, and more so nowadays social media posting. Online was always going to present several benefits to recruiters which primarily included cost savings, immediacy, and range. There was also going to be a greater degree of control over the posting process itself and the ability to change content on what was a living and breathing platform rather than having to make commitments to print runs which would then be set in stone in subsequent publications. Furthermore, with social media, facilitated targeting has been of immeasurable value to organisations that are seeking to make their workforces more diverse, inclusive, and representative of society or areas of society that they aim to serve.

So, what does this mean for candidates? Well, in the first instance, a considerably greater flow of opportunity-related information. You do not need to purchase magazines or periodicals and search through them for available jobs any longer. In fact, you do not need to go anywhere. You can access publications online from your computer, and now of course your smartphone, and to go one step further, you can set up job alerts that will simply email you links of opportunities relating to your search criteria.

As a candidate though, do not get too hopeful about job alerts. Sometimes the jobs are relevant. But if you are using job titles, such as *Account Manager* or *Supervisor*, expect to have to flick through some irrelevant tosh. It is unfortunately one of the downsides but hopefully outweighed by the useful nuggets that do get effortlessly pinged onto your screen. Unfortunately, the pressures of volume do mean that the search tools that underpin them are configured to ignore some search terms if the number of returns is going to be too low. For example, you may find that you are being presented with jobs within a 50-mile radius instead of the 10-mile parameter you specified. The same thing happens with online insurance quotations, which often bear little relevance to the search criteria you selected. It is all about ensuring that there is volume at the top of any *funnel*. If that hacks you off as a candidate, tough titteroonies.

Once you have signed up and are affixed to your screen, some of these charlatans will take the opportunity to throw at you what they can. You never know – maybe you are fed up with being a *Financial Analyst* and fancy chancing your arm at *Midwifery*. Either way, if you click the advertisement, someone somewhere adds a bead onto their revenue string, or whatever other hi-tech methodology is currently being employed. Let us hope it will soon be a pin in a Max Frances doll (for which I would be seeking royalties, have no fear).

This is all great news for recruiters because it means that they can achieve volume at the top of their recruitment funnels. Now depending on which media are used, there may well be a discrepancy in relation to the quality of volume that can be achieved for individual roles. After all, if you are advertising for a position that has specific minimum requirements, *you have very little control over which candidates actually apply*.

Do not think for one moment that in being very clear about minimum requirements, candidates will pay strict attention. Nor might it necessarily impact their decision to submit their CVs or application forms. Come on now, we have all chanced our arm somewhat and blissfully glided over one or two essential criteria that we do not meet and applied anyway. Particularly seeing that it is likely to be sifted by a student with the attention span of a cocker spaniel puppy. I would think that, indeed, we all have.

Recruiters can build application forms with so-called *killer questions* that filter out candidates before the stage when they review the applications but do not count on them to actually tell the truth. It is just human nature.

So, it is great for the candidates that they have more opportunities being presented to them and it is also great for candidates that the ease of application for roles is so much more straightforward. With a number of job boards, you can select *quick apply* and be winging over your penchant for a role in a matter of seconds.

This however does present a certain degree of false promise for the candidate. It means that even if you are a stellar candidate, your application is likely to get lost in the noise of all the others who have also pressed *quick apply* and banged out their CV.

You see, at the other end, recruiters are simply looking for a target number of candidates or viable candidates to progress to the next stage. It may therefore mean that if a recruiter has already achieved their target number of applications at the initial stage, they may not even look at your application at all.

Now I know what you are thinking. That is mesmerically dim and cannot possibly fulfil the aims and objectives of securing the best talent for organisations and clients of organisations. But please let me reiterate. Most recruiters are mesmerically dim, following self-defeating and mesmerically dim processes. It is not about attracting the best talent. It is about attracting numbers. Sufficient numbers. Volumes that will, with prevalent conversion ratios at each stage, provide enough hires of people who are suitably qualified to do the job.

Modern recruitment is the epitome of *satisficing*. Just doing enough to keep people happy while making as much money as possible. It has very little to do with excellence. Make no mistake, recruiters will secure the services of stellar and excellent candidates. But more often than not, it will be down to luck rather than judgement.

Once you have applied, you are, unbeknown to yourself, a number in a *pipeline*. Each stage of that *pipeline* will have a target number of applicants to reach and an expected pass rate for whatever test is put in front of you. And whether you succeed or fail at each test stage even if you manage to get into the funnelled *pipeline*, this will not necessarily be a matter of pure performance on your part.

Everything is relative and the benchmarks set that determine progression to subsequent stages will always be dependent on what that requirement is at that next stage. If there are 100 candidates in total and the organisation needs to progress 50, everyone will be ranked, and the pass mark will generally be set between the score of candidate 50 and that of candidate 51.

The benchmarks will therefore move up and down accordingly, relative to the performance of the cohort taking that particular test. So, a candidate who applies for a position will always have a greater chance of progressing if there are a higher number of vacancies ultimately available. Of course, it is logical and common sense, but only if you look at these processes from a purely mathematical or statistical perspective. As candidates, you are led to believe that your best is required, and you naturally go into these processes with the intention to do your best in the hope that your talent will shine through. That unfortunately does not always become the deciding factor.

With a lot of these volume processes, you may be asked to submit a CV at the beginning of your application, along with other details about your work experience and track record. In most cases, this information is not considered at any stage of the process, with all decisions up to the interview decided on psychometric test performance at however many stages are decided.

The CV is then typically brought into play when it is included in a candidate pack for the assessment panel. So, if you were under the impression that a volume recruitment process based on psychometric tests was purely objective and related to ability, just be very clear that it is a statistical numbers game up to the interview itself, at which point you will be susceptible to all manner of procedural flaws and subjective judgement.

Sorry to be the bearer of bad news, but it is not all flowers and sunshine in the world of volume recruitment. At least it is likely to be statistically more favourable than a process dependent on the cursory subjective review of the CV sifter.

There are however occasions in volume recruitment processes, particularly for so-called experienced hires, when the CV sift will be the very first stage in the process in order to clarify that a certain level of industry experience and know-how is under the belt of the candidates who progress.

This avoids the situation of candidates who can demonstrate competencies in diverse backgrounds being put forward for specialist roles where they need to hit the ground running. I can recall an application process where a client was looking for people with retail experience and did not have a CV sift in the process at all.

As a result, candidates with backgrounds such as working in circuses and flipping hamburgers were deemed to have passed the different competency stages, but clearly, they were not up to the hands-on selling and promotion of electrical equipment within a retail environment. This is probably the one occasion, where a CV sift would have been indispensable. I do understand, however, that the agency running that process did experience one of the more interesting first monthly reviews with their rather less than dissatisfied client. The *HR Director* wore the agency *Account Manager* like a novelty slipper. It was a steadfast example of how all great theories should be moderated with a touch of pragmatism.

§

One question that does arise about application processes concerns the timing of your submission. It should not matter at all and often it does not. But it can.

There are no hard and fast rules, but the following might help to guide you:

If the role is openly advertised, with a submission deadline, take as long as you like before that date. The recruiter will be looking to create a *funnel*, and everybody will be included in the mix. You will likely face some sort of online testing in the first few weeks after the deadline.

If the advertisement is open-ended, do not apply immediately. There is no advantage because they will not be making a decision straight away until they have a fair few candidates to benchmark. Apply too early and you run the risk of being an also-ran. Leave it for ten to fourteen days – possibly longer – after which some of the stronger candidates may have gone forward and been rejected. That way, you can feed on the increasing desperation of the recruiter (who will work harder for you) and the hiring manager (who is becoming more stressed at having not yet filled their pressing gap).

At this stage, any overall benchmarking goes out of the window and earlier candidates are already forgotten. You go straight into the leading pack.

As I said, not entirely scientific, but something to consider when applying.

§

Finally, as a candidate, you do need to understand that the trade-off for this ease of application and availability of opportunity will be a higher level of rejection.

Do not look at these opportunities even if in black-and-white they look to be the perfect job and start to get your hopes up. The overwhelming likelihood is that you will be rejected for these positions, and sadly, you will never know why. Often you will never even be told that you have been rejected, and you run the risk of whistling in the wind forever more, should you attempt to prise out some rationale for the decision on your application.

My personal advice would be, if a follow-up email is not successful, to draw a line under any role where you have not heard anything for four weeks. In fact, for most job boards which are not public sector roles, you can probably forget it if you have not heard after two weeks. Public sector recruitment is slightly different in that you will generally tend to see a higher level of transparency because these organisations are accountable for spending public money. As a result, they need to be seen to be giving value for money to members of the public, which understandably includes candidates.

Should you have a poor experience with a public sector organisation, there are a lot more trees you can shake and a lot more people you can piss off, should you decide to complain. That is not to say that these organisations do not make mistakes or never provide a poor service – anybody who has ever applied to the *Civil Service* or to a *Local Government* organisation will, I am sure, readily attest to that.

However, they have a greater sense of responsibility and accountability than your average blue-chip organisation in the private sector. As a candidate, I would always encourage you to hit public sector organisations hard if they showed signs of dragging their feet, non-response, or generally poor service.

At the end of the day, it will be the one area where you have a greater chance of pushing through and getting a result in the event that a mistake is made. Getting redress from private sector organisations regarding a recruitment foul-up will always be an uphill challenge unless you are fortunate enough to be in possession of some hard evidence.

But I would always recommend pushing it, if only to spin them somewhat and see where it goes. Sometimes their ineptitude in response becomes a more egregious matter than any mistake they might have made, particularly when they advance versions of events that are so obviously based on fiction. You never know, it might reach a point where you are just put through in order to sweep the mess under the carpet.

Think that that would be outrageous and unconscionable? Well, yes.

But then again, it's all starting to look that way, isn't it?

9 – Do Not Mention the War. I Mentioned It Once, and I Think I Got Away with It!

The War for Talent

Now I am sure there will be a lot of heads shaking at my statements that *'recruiting the best talent is impossible'*. Hardly surprising though in an industry where the most flippant of soundbites can become sacred cows that nobody dares challenge, let alone stun-bolt. People engaged in recruitment activities thrive on crap that they pick up from Twitter until somebody outside of the collective echo chamber challenges it and then everybody drops it like a £10 bag during a bust. Until the next time somebody with 100,000 followers is sitting on the Tube and half-asleep cranks out an unthinking tweet; and within a week, everyone in recruitment has appropriated another piece of *bo-lax*. It is how the obsession with *artificial intelligence (AI)* started and of course plummeted just as dramatically. As the Germans say:

'Als Tiger gesprungen, als Bettvorleger gelandet'.

Or roughly translated, *'Jumped like a tiger, landed like a rug'.* I will explore the recruitment bandwagons later, but back to the controversial statement that will have wanker recruitment *CEOs* shaking with anger down to their tan brogues (without socks, of course).

Let me unpack the statement about *'recruiting the best talent'* for a moment. What I am saying is that at the point an advertisement for a role hits the market, it would be ludicrous to suggest that the very best people out there who could do the job will actually ever even see the advertisement in the first instance. Anyone who suggests that they would is suggesting something that is statistically 100% implausible.

So therefore, it strikes me at the very first hurdle that it would be an uphill challenge — akin to a pushing-water-up-a-hill-with-a-fork kind of challenge — to suggest that any organisation would get the best talent for any job they chose to advertise.

At this stage, I could just drop the mic and move on to the next chapter. But when you have got those tossers over a barrel, you might as well move in with your Swarfega-lubed rooter and finish the job.

Pause.

Figuratively speaking, of course.

All they can ever shoot for is framing an advertisement that attracts people to apply who might be suitable for the role or who at least might possess some of the attributes required. From there, to put in place a process that clearly discerns the harvested wheat from the chaff so that the comparatively larger number of applications can be whittled down to a shortlist and ultimately an appointment.

For me, that is a sensible deduction.

That would translate into a process that, at best, hired somebody good enough to do the job. It absolutely could not be interpreted as a process that got the '*very best talent*'. That would be a ludicrous and hyperbolic assessment of any recruitment team's achievements. Even with the best of intentions (which arguably I do not have), to quote an oft-cited word, that would be somewhat *'punchy'*.

Amazing how these words arrive in the organisational lexicon. *'Punchy'*. If you think it is the kind of word that a fatuous wanker would use, you would be right.

But on with our dissection of this wonderfully baseless appropriation of the almost supernatural ability to produce advertisements, to which all the best and only the best people will respond.

In fact, the whole process of attracting great talent is largely a question of posting features of the opportunity that would be equally attractive to mediocre or even poor candidates because they would be to those who might ultimately be considered great. This is because ultimately people are interested in roles for three central reasons:

Firstly salary. Whatever people do say, salary has to be critical because people would not accept a job with a salary that was lower than the outgoings to which they have already made commitments. And while there is a delightfully disingenuous strand of bullshit that candidates like to adopt when discussing opportunities with the recruiters and prospective employers, i.e. that salary is not a key driver, or that they haven't really thought about it, the acceptance of any offer will invariably come down to salary and other compensation.

Of course, some organisations do not advertise salaries at all. And they do this for one reason only – to keep them open to being able to rip you off later in the process. It is not rude to ask about money, but it is rude to not offer the information upfront. Salary ranges should be tight, and certainly not more than 10% difference in the range for non-Executive-level roles. Wider, and they are likely to be harvesting or are not close enough to the job in question.

If you do get further in the process, there are unscrupulous employers out there who hope that you will be so invested in the role that you will be sufficiently psychologically weakened and more susceptible to a lower offer. Do not get sucked in people, it is a murky world out there.

Secondly, people look at location, which either needs to be suitable for commitments they have already made or compatible with lifestyle and family arrangements if they are indeed prepared to make changes.

And finally, it is the work itself. Because no matter how good the salary is, people still need to feel that they will be able to stick it, day in and day out.

So, if you are making clear what is on offer under those three elements – and I accept that depending on the candidate and circumstances they may prioritise any one of those differently in relation to the others – you will attract applications to your position, whether good, bad, or ugly.

No matter how many crazy gimmicks or pieces of creative you put up in front of your audience, people will still look for those three factors. And if you think that people will only look at a funky piece of creative before they will take notice of an available job, over perhaps something is purely textually based, then you are living in a dream world. Most likely a dream world where you are a *Creative Director* or some other person who believes that their existence will be justified by their levels of creativity until they are brought back down to earth by *Financial Directors*, who will tell you that creative is nonsense unless it sells.

So, all these *Directors* who talk about the *War for Talent* are essentially pushing forth verbosity through their collective rosebuds.

The main drivers for people to apply to an organisation for a role, once they have digested compensation, location, type of work etc will come down to two factors. And neither of those two will involve running through the *Crystal Maze* or being presented with a branded baseball cap. Those two factors will simply be either or perhaps both their own experience as a customer of that organisation or the reputation of that organisation that they get through interaction with others.

In fact, it is the one point where I am *somewhat* in agreement with recruitment marketers, namely when they talk about *Employer Value Propositions* or *EVPs*. It is just that I think it is a basic element of common sense rather than an overworked piece of *bullshido*, more suited to somebody's *HRM Diploma* coursework portfolio.

For the part of organisations, it is hard to believe that they fall for the tripe that is churned out by recruiters and those who are promoting employer brands, and in truth I am not too convinced that they do fall for it. It is just that there is a game of sorts, and businesses feel that they have to be part of it, or they will be left behind in the consciousness of candidates.

It is therefore not really about all the whizzy creative concepts that get put into practice under the guise of securing the best talent, it is about maintaining a presence in the market. If a graduate fair is taking place, then all the top blue-chip brands need to be represented in order to maintain the message that they are an option and should be considered. It actually doesn't matter what they are saying too much, over and above being clear on salary, where people we will be working and the type of work specialisms on offer. All the creative bollocks and the razzamatazz of the marketing tosspots trying to justify their petty existences will not cut the mustard with your average candidate. They know that it is all insubstantial froth and bubble.

As long as the candidates know that the opportunities are there, the applications will flow through, and they will be of variable quality as they are for all roles within all organisations. End of.

I mean it is a rather bizarre proposition that the underlying message that advertising agencies suggest to their clients is that the greatest creative concepts will attract the best talent. Or that the use of advanced technology like *AI* would achieve the same results. It is absolute nonsense.

All you are achieving is making yourself more noticeable, or you are potentially facilitating channels where you become more noticeable. It is a volume game that has no bearing on the quality of those who go on to express an interest or apply for your positions. All you are doing is increasing the numbers at the top of the *funnel* but not necessarily increasing the probability that great candidates will appear at the bottom.

It is all about creating the illusion of usefulness and differentiation. Which I kind of get because people can hardly say, *'we are a volume-based business that will help you to sift through the useless tossers to enable you to uncover the odd genius'.* It is just not inspiring.

§

And it is also not as lucrative as getting people to pay for expertise. Anyone can hire a grunt for the minimum wage. But if you want to secure high levels of revenue, then you need to be offering something a little more special. This is however all about show. It is all about demonstrating to everybody, not just to potential candidates, that you are operating at the *cutting edge*. Do not be deluded into thinking that any of this caper translates into a better quality of person entering the organisation, or any of the recruitment organisations themselves being anything more than cost-cutters and volume grinders. They are not.

With your standard job postings, it is a question of grabbing the attention of the candidates, so they apply. Now you may choose to have a very creative graphic and make the posting less text-heavy.

Bravo, give that over-hyped Liberal Democrat a cigar. But what you are doing is grabbing attention. If you can then hold that, by being clear on what the benefits are, you will get applications – which will include the whole range and gamut of dross, mediocrity, and brilliance.

If at the end of the process, some really good candidate is hired and the hiring manager or client is very pleased with that, they may well draw the conclusion that they have hired some great talent.

And at that point, why not pull out the Cava and pop a cork?

However, once you delve into the details and analyse what has actually happened, there is aptly no evidence to suggest that the advertisements or the content of the advertisements was necessarily ever going to attract great talent, per se.

For Christ's sake, do us all a favour and stop pretending that it would.

There is nothing in that kind of approach that establishes a causal link between successfully targeting the very best people, who then go on to make an application. Nevertheless, for many years, the fat cats in the recruitment advertising industry have been dining out on this, or rather on the fact that nobody really takes the trouble to go back and question whether something might have happened by pure chance.

This is an outcomes-based industry and therefore, if good hires are achieved, you can bet your bottom Euro that those in recruitment advertising will absolutely be connecting client satisfaction with their unique abilities. They have been trumpeting a kind of pseudoscience for years.

And in some ways, you can understand why they will take the credit if so many people are prepared to allow them to do so, without challenging it with any factual evidence. Maybe you just have to let these people have their little moment of glory. After all, it would not be in the interests of client organisations to belittle the efforts of agencies who, albeit fortuitously, do at least something that makes a contribution to the candidate pipeline.

But in actual fact, all job postings do is attract interest and volume. Granted, the right balance of graphics and text allows candidates' attention to be gained and for there to be sufficient factual information that may prompt an application. And I have absolutely no issue in accepting that there is skill in designing job advertisements for that very purpose.

However, let us not get too carried away and equate this with the ability to design advertisements that attract great talent. It is absolute nonsense, completely bereft of any rational justification.

In practice, the majority of job advertisements that you are likely to see as a candidate will be poorly written, often with discriminatory copy that will more likely than not turn you off the role in question, or they will contain so much cliched terminology that you will not really understand what the job poster is seeking.

Of course, sometimes that is intentional in order to serve as a coded form of language for internal candidates and to provide suitable hooks on which to hang their ill-fitting pinhead hats when it comes to establishing a rationale for regretting any external candidates unfortunate enough to have wasted time with an application.

That is, on the other hand, not to say that some of those in the sphere of recruitment marketing are not able to make good on the promise of attracting great talent. But there is only one sure-fire way to achieve this. And that is through the expert delivery of a strategy underpinned by *content marketing*.

§

So, what is *content marketing* and how does it relate to recruitment advertising? Well, in essence, it is a kind of marketing that is driven by the creation of material that is shared online – blogs, videos, and various other social media posts, to name but a few – that do not per se advertise specific positions, but which highlight the credibility of organisations and their products and services.

The principal idea that sits behind this is the strategic building of audiences. Now, let us have a closer look at what we mean by *an audience*. You see, many of the recruitment marketing agencies out there will absolutely be doing all of this content-sharing via any available channel they can get their grunts piped into. There is no shortage of blogs and shared articles that are spewed forth by the marketing departments of such organisations. And it is largely shit. Pure unadulterated number two.

In fact, we are positively drowning in piss-poor, faecal content, if that is not a contradiction in terms.

Much of this, is simply the fruits of seemingly endless trawls online to find articles that may well have some bearing on whatever subject is being floated. Much of this is then often posted out of context and with minimal insight from organisations, in terms of how they are bringing that to light and making it relevant. You need to realise that the expertise that most of these social media recruitment droids possess is that they have a *Facebook* account, or they have shared the odd *tweet*. They are generally post-adolescent sub-employees in their first paid positions. They do not even know how to give a shit.

Accordingly, they do not build a relevant audience through this activity that will facilitate the introduction of their products and services and most importantly for this context, their job postings. They are in effect hijacking collateral which, from a strategic perspective, does not build an *engaged audience*. People are not reading these articles and concluding that the organisation posting them is one with whom they would want to link up.

These recruitment advertising organisations take on the role of some crusty old busker rather than some major star for whom you pay good money to see. I quite like the image of the busker because these recruitment advertisers are just riding in the slipstream of those with real talent. They learn a few skills and think that they can trot out their tunes, being completely oblivious to the fact that people just do not hang around, let alone part with their readies.

The thing about musicians is that to be successful, you need to either be original or do great covers. Most in this business manage neither.

You see, great content marketers have clear objectives before they even put pen to paper for the very first time. These experts demonstrate through a corpus of intellectually stimulating and values-based content the real essence of what organisations stand for and are seeking to achieve through their products and services. In doing so, they build an audience of people who are similarly *engaged* and who are *at the right level intellectually* to appreciate this and to *take discussions to an even higher level*.

Once this kind of relationship has been established with audiences, it is then a question of clarifying all the more tangible benefits for prospective employees and of course, to have a reputation in the marketplace where other like-minded professionals will corroborate that the organisation is a worthy one.

This is the only way that recruitment advertising activity can be deemed to attract great talent. But it is not attracting great talent through a one-hit advertisement. It is about engagement and relationship-building because ultimately the only people who subsequently apply through these channels are the ones who understand and appreciate the depth and breadth of organisations rather than focusing purely on benefits and convenience.

The problem for us as candidates is that the vast majority of content marketing is done without any strategic forethought and is simply the result of poseurs and pretenders, who are jumping on the bandwagon and trying to position themselves as so-called *thought leaders* and *experts*.

As a result, this type of activity serves to do nothing other than use up some more bandwidth for whatever tosh they are peddling via their websites. You see this most often on social media sites where these so-called *recruitment marketers* use social media simply to post direct advertisements for their jobs so that social sites effectively become alternative job boards.

Now that is not to say that this has entirely no uses because it does allow organisations to get roles out there and points jobs to specific target groups who are active on social media. That may have a role in terms of helping to promote some areas of diversity within the candidate cohorts. But by electing only to *promote tweets*, for example, or just by sharing, these impostors are in effect not grasping the most effective ways of using the extensive online tools that are available to marketers. It is a little like using an electric drill to hammer in a screw.

They just do not get it.

But in many ways, the failure to take on board the essence of content marketing is down to the senior managers, who have not appreciated how advertising has changed so much in the last 20 years.

 Some of these people have only just survived the switch from print advertising to online advertising and it took them so long to adjust that they are now failing to distinguish between online postings and all the versatility of social media – and how it can be used to support candidate attraction strategies that really do lead to an uplift in quality applications.

It certainly does prompt a chortle or two when you hear these outlandish claims of one-dimensional job posters that their tedious and uninspiring job postings generate quality candidates. Particularly when the capability to achieve this often exists within their own organisations but never gets operationalised because the senior managers who are stuck in the ancient world of print, simply do not understand the concepts.

Better the bullshit you know, I suppose.

§

I suppose much of what I have said about what attracts people to organisations is often summed up by marketing bullshitters as an *employer value proposition* or *EVP*. I mentioned this particular strain of vacuous twaddle earlier. Essentially an *EVP* reflects the values and culture, such as learning growth and development opportunities, that will be practical benefits for a potential employee. It has gained a lot of credence because organisations are beyond shit-scared that when they do need outside talent, people will elect not to join them.

Therefore, in time-honoured tradition, everything needs to be rolled up into a nice and handy concept that can be added to web content and job advertisements that splendidly sums up what you will get in exchange for joining any particular organisation. It is about the unique set of benefits that an employee receives in return for the skills, capabilities, and experience that they bring to a company. This is then beefed up by lashings of additional dressing that encompass the mission statement and why that is important to the outside world, why the EVP is inspirational, and what employees get from being part of it.

But in all honesty, apart from some people who will have moralistic reasons why certain organisations are unacceptable, *does any of this really matter?* What actually matters is just a bit of common sense to highlight what the offerings are. If *EVPs* were just that, then I'd be in.

And the answer to the *'does it really matter?'* question is of course, no. People join organisations because they need to earn money, the role is close enough to them that it will not disrupt their lifestyle, and the nature of the role is something that they could do without too much of a stretch. Even those individuals who are seeking advancement will be more than happy to take on a role for a particular period of time while they either look around for other opportunities or explore whether there is the potential for progression within the enterprise in which they have just landed.

Just let that sink in for a moment.

Everything that I have just said here is about pragmatism. People are nothing if not pragmatic. When you get down to the basics of the real recruitment game, recruiters are pragmatic. Unfortunately, candidates are frequently not. You see what happens is that organisations and recruiters have to participate in a certain amount of playacting in order to meet the norms of everyday commercial life. That is to say, you have to be demonstrating that you are pushing the boundaries and doing things that are new and that are innovative, whereas in reality what is actually happening is simply a question of what I would call *'adequate placement'*.

But to make everything as attractive as possible to the consumers at different levels, there needs to be a performance. You can order crêpes at a restaurant, but that is not as exciting as when the waiter flambées them at the side of the table. It is the theatre and the performance, which for some people translates as something better or more enjoyable. But at the end of the day, it is still the same pancake that could have been made in the kitchen and collected from the pass.

In our minds, if we see something flashy that is conceptualised, we immediately justify our own decision to purchase the product or service. All those arguments about the expense and all those doubts that we may have had evaporated into the air like, dare I say, the steam from my flambée. And I have to say, there are not many recruiters out there to whom I would give the steam from my flambée.

So, you know, if you work for a recruiting organisation, or if a recruiter is trying to sell you the *EVP* that they will *'build'* (yes, that is really how they do position it) that will help you to attract great talent, just remember that it would be an incredible proposition for them to suggest that any buildable concept would lead to the attraction of better talent.

Without a doubt, it might brighten up your web content, but when all is said and done, you will get applications based on salary, convenience, and the nature of the work. Everything else, people will treat as secondary. Let us be frank, everybody knows that organisational life is not a bed of roses and that wherever you go, there will be your motley crew of arseholes, dysfunctional departments, a lack of processes and general foolery.

Do not try and dress up everything to appear whiter than white because, at the end of the day, the candidates are just not buying it. In fact, they are not even submitting it to anything more than cursory consideration. In fact, in a world where there are so many over-egged *EVPs*, all saying effectively the same thing, none of them would stand out even if it were a laudable concept.

I do know of one example though, where a recruitment agency-cum-RPO helped a client with *EVP*, got involved in all the seemingly endless bullshit of theme days and awards entries, all wonderfully branded, with as many coloured pens, badges, and rosettes you could shake a stick at. You name it, they were doing it and billing a fortune.

And all the photos, videos and posters were being spaffed over every social media channel you could possibly conceive. All signed off because the principal contact within the hiring organisation was seeking the coveted title of *Director*. As weak and nun's piss and not just an imposter but an imposter doing business with imposters.

The whole set-up was like an imposter Russian doll. Every time you peeled away a layer of the context, another imposter popped out.

The whole enterprise was simply geared towards blowing a perpetual stream of smoke up the arse of an inconsequential and useless tosser with the actual candidates left to go whistle.

The solitary shining achievement of the exercise has in fact been that it has exemplified everything that is plastic in recruitment land.

As the veritable cherry on top, the shitebox RPO made his principal contact an unqualified internal appointment who had failed the internal application process but was still shoehorned into the role. A clusterfuck that symbolised the absolute hypocrisy of recruitment practice. But it'll never stop while mugs are out there willing to pay for it.

So, while all this tomfoolery was unfolding in the background, and people were poncing about in their branded t-shirts and picking up their glass globes for 'best turd' or whatever accolades they were bestowing upon each other, the actual service (yes, the actual practice of undertaking recruitment activities and the essential reason for the existence of these enterprises) was just banging any old candidate through the process, often bypassing agreed protocols. Candidates were waiting for 4 weeks for responses to their queries if receiving them at all. Several pass/fail decisions were incorrectly made, good candidates were wrongly failed, and poor ones were getting hired even though they had failed the assessment. Nobody really cared about applying any kind of quality control. The recruitment lead in the agency could scarcely cope and for a long while spent afternoons sobbing in the toilet.

But there were huge billings and very low costs. Lots of social media sharing and the client got promoted to their bullshit *'Director'* role. The brand inevitably suffered among candidates, but this remained closed off to the wider world, owing to the control that RPOs can frequently weald over perceptions. A classic *private vs public* situation, and we will explore this in just a little more detail further on in Chapter 15.

As matters stand, the turds have not yet floated to the top of the bowl. Yet.

Until then, everyone's a winner and everything, the whole shoddy fake enterprise, still looks great on paper. But none of it contributes to *great talent*.

And when it all breaks down, who are they going to call?

Scambusters?

Well, what will happen is that people will already have moved on, with some great stories to tell on their CVs. The only saving grace is that nobody is likely to give that more than a cursory glance! What irony. What a time to be alive.

§

So now back to that wonderful concept, The *War for Talent*, first formulated by a management consultant Stephen Hankin in 1997[v], who was responding to the challenges posed by demographic shifts that impacted adversely on the balance between supply and demand.

There is no definition of *talent*, other than the expression, like *obscenity*, 'that you will know it when you see it', presumably in whatever the relevant context is.

In the modern world of recruitment, the phrase exists rather blandly to exemplify the challenges of recruitment organisations primarily to run successful attraction campaigns, which we have now explored. It could also be expanded to the part of the process where organisations go on to make the most of valid and reliable assessment tools to identify (and appoint) the best in the pipeline once they have applied. We will explore this in more detail later on when we examine the *Funnel* and the various assessment tools. But be warned – their case doesn't get any stronger!

Understandably, recruiters want to characterise the work they do as being of high quality, which reasonably they would want to equate to having produced higher quality candidates into the pipelines.

It is undoubtedly a fundamentally nonsensical argument if organisations have at the very least included in their advertisements the necessary components that all candidates seek. And even if you were to produce solely textual advertisements, you would still attract the right level of interest that ultimately would enable you to *satisfice* the client requirement. That is to say, hire people who are good enough to do the job or jobs that are available.

But let us not deny the recruiters their little guilty pleasures. If they were unable to see themselves as *Field Marshals* on the battlefield of talent, they would be unable to strategise in their *thought leadership blogs* that they so diligently scrape together after their personal assistants have successfully logged them into *their PCs* every morning.

Let them live in their worlds, where they convince themselves that all the activity that helps their marketing teams generate the waves of abysmal content is actually worthwhile.

Meanwhile, candidates can reassure themselves that no, they are not losing their minds when they read some of this abject nonsense, which resonates not one iota with their experiences of the marketplace.

Rest assured, that all this rubbish is all window dressing. Do not feel panicked that you are in competition with great talent. You are simply going for roles that a whole host of other people also need in order to make a realistic living.

Take the pressure off yourself and remember that the people who are running the recruitment exercises to which you are applying are simply churning numbers. Spot the warning signs, and if you do decide to submit your CV or your application, make sure that the amount of effort you put into it is commensurate with the likelihood of success.

Do not get sucked into the mindset that this is some innovative ultra-professional process, where the rules are fair and where your talent will earn its just reward.

It is grim out there and everything is hyped up to the extent that your self-worth can be unduly diminished. Do not let it happen.

And just don't mention the war. We won't let you get away with it.

10 – Wagons Role!

Artificial Intelligence (AI) and the irresistible lure of bandwagons

For those of you (unfortunate enough to have been) well-versed in dealing with contact centres, you will doubtless have seen the swing from voice-centric customer communications to email and latterly chat. You see contact centres have for many years concerned themselves with what they like to term *channel-switching*. That is to say, encouraging customers to communicate in ways that are more efficient and more effective for the contact centres themselves to organise a suitable response.

You see, the thing with inbound telephone calls is that it is very difficult to anticipate when they might arrive, and very challenging to ensure that resource is always cost-effectively allocated at the right points in the day. Therefore, email is a favoured form of communication, for the contact centres at least because they can allocate the work themselves to times when they have people available to respond to customers. In some cases, organisations seek to avoid customer contact altogether, by running processes powered by AI, which read a customer email before the customer even has the chance to send it via a contact form. This suggests possible answers to the query by pushing online articles to the customer before they even press <send> and of course by definition so that the organisation does not actually have to answer. This is known as reducing *avoidable contact or deflecting contact.*

Unsurprisingly, customers absolutely loathe this by and large, not just because the articles that are suggested are often irrelevant, but because customers are led to believe they are about to send a communication, and it becomes apparent that organisations were intending all along that they would not be able to do this. For the contact centres, this approach has now morphed into a clear interest in chat-based solutions, for several reasons.

Firstly, organisations have realised that one agent can deal with up to 10, maybe even 15 chats at the same time, so while there is certainly more immediacy involved with chat in comparison with email, this can be more than compensated by a considerable increase in agent multi-tasking. Organisations that have moved towards chat have bolstered efficiencies by incorporating AI into the chat process and having bots running in the background that can either answer frequently asked questions themselves or filter down customer queries so that the chats can then be directed to the most appropriately trained adviser to deal with specific problems.

So, it was never going to be long before recruitment organisations jumped on the bandwagon of AI. The consumption of positive case studies in one volume setting was always going to be attractive for others in the volume universe. Naturally, that meant *recruiters* too.

Lamentably but not surprisingly, recruiters did not need to consume or digest too much factual detail before espousing AI with some gusto. It was a whirlwind romance. In fact, they skipped the whole courtship and went straight to the cigarette.

In the recruitment world, if something smells like it may have cash attached, they are in, seated and with their proverbial popcorn ready. No question of even the slightest hesitation, they have seen the dust clouds in the distance, the whole posse is whipped up, and they are on that wagon. After all, if you are not on the recruitment bus, somebody will throw you under it.

You then have to watch the excruciating charade, delivered à la school play, by executives struggling to make sense of the printouts from *the Web* provided by their PAs, on why AI is the way forward.

Almost as painful as when *Diversity* was king. All those fat, middle-aged white men in 30-year-olds' fashion talking about how they loved black people and gays.

Sometimes even women were mentioned.

Those were heady days indeed.

Of course, diversity is still big though not as big since we saw an increased threat of Islamic-related terrorism. The genii in agencies and RPOs struggled for quite a while with that one, to reconcile this with their commitment to diversity. Such is the shallow capability of their collective reason. AI was a bandwagon that, being inextricably linked to pound notes, they have had to get onto.

So, for years, it has been difficult to have any conversation with somebody in the world of outsourced recruitment at least, without them mentioning AI and how it is going to revolutionise their industry. The problem with the recruitment business is that it saw the emergence of some funky technology and was desperate to think of ways in which it could incorporate that into its offering.

Rather than following the most successful strategic approach of, erm, successful technology companies, they start with the needs of the customer and then explore how technology might best support the customer journey in order to improve service delivery.

I have lost count of the number of times people in the recruitment business have introduced AI into the conversation with customers, only for it to transpire that they did not have any product in place to support the amazing pitches they were putting forward. You see them unravel in minutes. It is quite something.

It has been abjectly embarrassing to see the usual procession of pompous, puffed-up recruitment *Account Directors* instigating impromptu pitches on how they want to introduce you to chatbots, only for everyone to discover, with minimal probing, that there has been nothing real in place behind it at all.

I mean, actually nothing. Pure hot air. In fact, after a probing, it became clear that expertise went as deep as, well, just raising the question of AI and having a chat. Presumably, the plan would be to hand over to a third party to deliver a solution and then to skim off a tidy percentage with some more account management time. Who knows, but I never saw one realistic pitch or anything tangible get off the ground.

You see, these people who gas off about AI, like demented, buzzword-razzed Greta Thunbergs are what you might call '*actorvists*'. Pretend activists. You see, they do not own chatbot technology. They have never made any investment in it and never thought it through in terms of how it would work. But they fire off their soundbites to any shit-kicking lightweight who has the time to listen.

They haven't even twigged that not only do you need to invest, but you have to invest separately for each of the organisations you support. You cannot just buy a bot and roll it out throughout your business. You have to develop and 'train' them, which is going to be very different for each direct recruitment context supported. They just do not get it, but it doesn't stop Billy Bullshit executives, while adjusting their ill-fitting *Armani* frames on their expansive heads, from telling any old turd ad nauseam *that 'the future of recruitment will be chatbots communicating with clients etc'.*

Like Greta, these incorrigible berks need to get back to school and finish their education.

You wonder why they are promoting artificial intelligence in the first instance when not even possessing the real thing.

You see for recruitment agencies, the discussions on AI are simply a classic advertiser ploy. To attract investor attention, just as their job advertisements attract candidate attention. It is not about improving the quality of service, it is just about trying to get a seat at the table, by feigning higher-level involvement in high-profile activities.

Now I am not sure whether any recruiter out there has actually progressed to the use of bots or any other AI substitute for human interaction, aside from automated test marking and the use of conditional steps in online application forms (all standard for years). But what I can tell you, as a candidate, is that you should be steering clear of any organisation that promotes this kind of dross and thinks that it is an acceptable way to deal with professionals, at the point that the candidates might make be making a life-changing decision about their employment status.

And similarly speaking, if you see any recruitment organisation giving serious credence to the use of this kind of functionality, you should avoid them like the plague. What does it tell you about how they value you as a candidate, who might have serious concerns, worries, anxieties, or questions about what is likely to be one of the single most important decisions you make at any given time?

And that is that they do not care very much at all.

Surely, personable, empathetic, and expert candidate support is essential for any organisation seeking to engage and recruit? You would hope so. But just as recruiters infer all sorts of conclusions from you, you are entitled to apply the same logic from them. And it does not make good reading.

AI bot usage would confirm what you doubtless already suspect of recruiters you have encountered. You are simply a number that can be dealt with automatedly, like all the other numbers out there. To them, you are nobody special but a statistic on a *pipeline report*.

There is not one shed of compassion or empathy being offered by an organisation, that would allow an off-the-shelf computerised response to be given to what is a bespoke and very personal concern that you might have. Half of these companies who bang on about AI would absolutely put these kinds of solutions into practice if they had any idea on how such solutions could be effectively operationalised.

The truth is though, that most of these dimwits do not have a clue at all about AI or most other emerging technologies for that matter. I know of volume recruiters still working off basic ATS systems and Outlook, who have not even made the investment in any integrated systems for their resourcing, reporting, or routing. They either do not understand the benefits or do not think that they are worth it.

It is likely to be a bit of both.

§

The fact that these recruitment bullshitters do consider chatbot interactions at all tells you more about these organisations and their motivations than any dire or out-of-context content some work experience marketing assistant has scraped off *Bing* and re-churned as *thought leadership*. It tells you that, aside from having IQs marginally in excess of the school dunce, they are vacant to the core. It reflects a lust for money, without any consideration of how it might serve the purpose they purport to have.

On with the cone and into the corner, you underwhelming, vacuous thought-vagrants.

It furthermore makes them, more so than simply a world apart from the images they seek to portray, staggeringly incompetent that they cannot even get these albeit unfeasible solutions off the ground. Or that they cannot realise that this technology needs alternative applications to allow it to complement and enhance customer objectives. Or that it is just not suited to this context because desired cost savings achieved via this route would disproportionately erode service.

The list of implications could be endless.

Any one of these would do though, chaps, but do yourselves a favour and jump off the bandwagon and onto something more creditable.

Maybe something you *believe in*.

You never know, you might add more to the debate by highlighting the limitations of AI in its current forms and providing some unique critical insight on your caution.

Just please step away from the platform right now. While I do at my most mischievous find it slightly entertaining, it has a cringe-comedy effect. Sometimes, I cannot bear to look.

But there is no denying that they are as incompetent as they are disingenuous. It is absolutely fine to have automated steps in a volume-based process, for example, if candidates are simply providing information or vice versa. Not only acceptable but also efficient for both sides for such processes to be in operation.

But as a substitute where empathy and understanding need to play key roles? Organisations that seriously go down this line are simultaneously providing candidates with some insight into life after hire. Once again, be careful people.

§

You may however be familiar with some recruitment solutions where other forms of automation are already in place, particularly at assessment centre stages, for example in the generation of feedback reports. In these circumstances, when assessors assign scores for specific competencies, these reports pull through fixed comments that are then used to populate fields in feedback templates for candidates.

The candidates then receive their feedback reports that ostensibly represent an assessor's view on how they did, which in fact are pre-determined generalisations, for example, of what a score of 1, 2 or 3 means.

Naturally, candidates would never know this because the homogeneity of comments would be discernible only through the comparison of a range of feedback reports, which naturally individual candidates never see.

It can also lead to some interesting situations during the final moderation stages if scores are factored up or down and the corresponding scores are not. You would hope that the reports would all be re-run in such cases in order to eliminate this risk. Sometimes I am sure they are, but I have personally witnessed when they have not been, and candidates have received feedback with incongruent scores and comments. For those, an already phoney process is further complicated by the obvious inconsistencies.

Is it any wonder that candidates lose faith? The next time you do receive one of these reports, see if you can hook up with a fellow candidate if you know one personally or are in touch via an online forum. Then compare your reports and see.

Be prepared for the sinking feeling of once again being let down by those who should know better.

Nonetheless, in receipt of such a report following a formal assessment, it should make you think again about how much the organisation concerned really cared about you as a candidate and how much stock they placed in the importance of feedback.

In case you are wondering, not much.

All they are doing is in fact simply implementing an automated process *to give the impression* that they are providing valuable feedback, whereas in fact they are simply going through the motions. I would encourage every candidate to take a step back and undertake an assessment of their own recruitment processes in which they are involved. Probe a little deeper and judge whether any of these automations are in place. If they are, you will get a greater insight into just how engaged these organisations really are, and how they are living up to the values they are so keen to trumpet in their corporate paraphernalia.

Getting this type of insight early doors may well save heartache in the future.

Of course, given the importance many companies place on critical thinking, which they are only too keen to test via one of their psychometric exercises, to which they attribute so much importance, you would hope that they would welcome such scrutiny.

However, such is their reliance on tests and processes, they completely lose touch with the real world. On the one hand, they are putting tests in front of candidates as valid and reliable means of testing their abilities and judgement, and yet on the other hand, they use these crass techniques and expect the very same candidates to accept them as consistent with the values they spray all over social media.

What a staggering deficiency in self-awareness.

But then again, like the PR industry, the recruitment industry is famous for not being able to take its own advice. They pride themselves on putting in place tools that will discern the strong from the weak and yet via their fanfare and self-indulgent celebrations of their brilliance, they communicate their own incompetence.

AI is the one that the *volume recruiters* cannot quite shake off. They committed to it early with such a splash that any backtracking has become an insurmountable challenge in itself.

It is like they have decided to ride a tiger and then are afraid to dismount. But it is the gift that keeps on giving, for those of us who like to see charlatans starting to initiate their own inexorable death wobble.

Every time something new on AI comes to the fore, they are not quite sure where to go. It says as much about their intentions as it does about their incompetence. They will do anything for a fact buck, anything. And screw those who get trampled underfoot. They are just collateral damage.

It is almost predictable though that even when they can use some automation in practice, apart from the very basics, it will negate the very purpose for which the process in question stands. The level of hypocrisy in recruitment never ceases to amaze and astound.

In many ways though, the blind money-lust of volume recruitment and its associated, bandwagon-obsessed hypocrisy has become the revolution that is eating its children.

Only time will tell, but client attrition is already starting to erode the empires of the larger players.

The doors on the saloons are swinging and the phones are now not always ringing.

11 – Funnel Vision

Pouring the numbers into the recruitment funnel

I referred to this notion earlier, so now time for the *big reveal*.

Well, not really.

I am sure that the mere mention of the term funnel, within the context of recruitment, was sufficient for all to grasp what was likely to be sketched out. It is worth a deeper delve though because it sits at the heart of any arguments against the absurd notion of recruiting 'the best talent'.

I have already explained why this preposterous soundbite is, well, precisely that from the word go when seeking to attract candidates. However, I do concede that the use of an in-depth content-based strategy will absolutely have a bearing on engagement with higher quality candidates who recognise in that content the features of a high-performing and virtuous organisation. Of course, embarking on such a contact strategy requires investment. Recruiters, being the revenue-hungry beasts that they are, are particularly averse to investments because they are spending money and incurring costs without being able to add corresponding revenue lines to the balance sheet.

Anybody who has ever worked for a recruitment agency or RPO will know that the most powerful person in the organisation will typically be the *CFO*. And the CFOs will frequently be qualified accountants, who indeed embody the principles of accountancy, in spirit as well as in deed. In brief, they are bean-counters who appreciate quantitative data but barely give a thought to anything that is more qualitative.

Strategic accounting? Yes. Strategic business and account management? Not in the slightest.

It is all about batting out some money and then getting something back in return. Why do you think *recruiters* and *RPOs* are so wedded to volume job postings? Why do you think their so-called *content marketers* are in fact simply posting jobs and links to semi-relevant articles? Because that's what they do.

They go for volume and hope that some of it sticks.

§

So, this brings us to the top of the funnel. Lots of numbers and candidates of varying capability and suitability. That my friends, is a fact. And this shortcut around having to invest immediately brings a downside.

That is to say, this large number of candidates needs to be whittled down to an acceptable or manageable level for the final round of assessment and then hire. This is not just a practical consideration but a commercial one as recruitment process unit costs become considerably more expensive as they progress. Therefore, the quantity of the units has to be reduced accordingly. Assessment centres (ACs), being typically the final stage of assessment (but not always because sometimes there is a final interview on top of that), exemplify this with the cost of facilities and more senior staff (together with opportunity cost) representing a considerable expense.

So how does the *funnel* work? Well, somewhere along the line an *HR Specialist* or an *Occupational Psychologist* will design a recruitment process with a number of separate testing stages, which will be *pass/fail* for candidates. And this is where it gets interesting. Primarily because each stage needs to be efficient as well as effective. Now ACs, or at least well-designed ACs, have a purported validity in that they comprise a number of exercises which allow for individual competencies to be tested more than once. That way, the evidence can be *triangulated*, and the assessors can be reasonably sure whether that has (or not) met the requirements of the competency. This is another reason why the AC stage garners a higher level of expenses. A lot more happens in them. At the earlier stages in the process, where there are more candidates, it is essential that whatever test process is selected, the individual unit costs for that process are lower.

So, the options for recruiters are to use automation where possible, quick reviews or single-dimension automation-enabled online tests. Therefore, at these early stages, you may have bespoke tests that are automatically assessed via computer, and which are not volume-sensitive in terms of units (but these will of course require upfront investments to design, which if not accepted by a hiring organisation, will not happen).

More common will be a cursory review of CVs, which take it from me will not involve more than 1 minute for each one on the part of a recruiter. Hardly a thorough assessment of candidate capability and again, wholly reliant on the capability and understanding of the reviewer. Most common, and of particular interest to volume recruiters, will be the use of online *psychometrics*. This will (often though not always) involve candidates being tested on individual dimensions, which will determine pass or fail, irrespective of their wider range of skills that might be pertinent to the role in question.

Already, you may be seeing some issues with this.

The savvier recruiters will try to ensure that there are a handful of tests that test a wider range of skills, which make this process just a little more accurate and, dare I say it, fairer. This is by no means the most typical scenario. Remember these recruiters are hellbent on maximising revenue and minimising costs in order to achieve maximum levels of margin.

Now this is not unusual for businesses, but most other rational businesses at least allow for a moderation of these drives in whatever direction, based on a recognition that quality of service is the raison d'être for their engagement in the first instance. Such considerations rarely permeate through to the thought processes of recruitment organisations though. Nonetheless, as a candidate, you will be more confident where those processes are designed and run by an internal recruitment function. That is because their decisions are likely to be supported by a senior management team that has customers closer to their hearts – and indeed may be subject to vigilance from a *Customer Experience Director* or some other person of that ilk. That is again why you must be very careful to ascertain the level of involvement from recruitment agencies and RPOs.

So, the sad fact is, Ladies and Gentlemen, even if the recruiter has invested significant amounts of money in their *content marketing* strategy (albeit that this is extremely unlikely), those quality candidates are likely to bite the dust at one of any number of different stages, for reasons completely unconnected with their suitability as candidates.

You couldn't make it up, could you? In these cases, it really is pulling defeat from the jaws of victory.

Needless to say, when that mix of candidates at the very beginning is based on a volume *'spray-and-pray'* philosophy, the likelihood of fantastic hires being squeezed out at the end of the process is even more diminished.

Added to this, the inability of organisations to effectively manage their *pipelines* and the situation becomes even worse. The higher the numbers and the lengthier the process, the more likely that candidates will be incorrectly processed and left behind. Candidates with *reasonable adjustments* will frequently not get them or will receive incorrect ones. If recruitment agencies or RPOs are involved, consider misprocessing a given, and it is possible that many of these incidents will never ever float to the surface.

For candidates like yourselves, you will for the most part have been none the wiser. I can enlighten you though that one of the most laughable situations behind the scenes is when *recruitment officers* are attempting to interpret the status of their pipelines to other stakeholders. This is because the health of a pipeline is determined by the overall conversion rate at each step, which while a campaign is running will naturally fluctuate. This forward projection of a combination of mathematical calculations will frustrate your average process manager to the point where their already restricted cerebral cortices will judder and stall with hilarious regularity.

As per the responsibilities of their office, they will distribute a management information report to their stakeholders and then be required to present progress. A review of what has happened so far, combined with a projection into the future. You can imagine the type of thing. Now, when you consider that the average *recruitment advisor* has the brain power of a cauliflower floret, the analysis of the simplest data is not going to be a breeze. Numbers that change daily will flick them into an immediate death wobble, with the prospect of the further calculations required for projection leading to grey matter paralysis and thought vaporisation.

So, they go onto these conference calls with clients and stakeholders, like lambs to the slaughter. Their only hope is that the more discerning attendees are absent, have to leave early, or are busy multi-tasking on the call and are not listening attentively. Many a poor soul I have seen eviscerated in less than a minute in those scenarios.

Those who try to muddle their way through will spend the ensuing discussion trying to work out, in tandem with those stakeholders, what it all means. Never a great situation to be in when you are supposedly the expert in the provision of a service. And if you think I am exaggerating this point, speak to somebody you know in the recruitment industry who has ever engaged an agency for a volume recruitment exercise. They will undoubtedly describe it in terms of the blind leading the blind. And that will be a polite articulation.

It is not all the fault of the indescribably hebetudinous and obtuse recruitment grunts, though. Almost certainly, they will be working from MI reports that would be more effectively compiled by preschool infants versed in the art of potato printing. And of course, in this context – and particularly when attempting to project results – *volume recruiters* betray the principal weakness of their approach to the activities they undertake. That is everything is based on numbers and statistical analysis. Or at least it would be if they were actually able to analyse the numbers in the first instance.

Stakeholders generally pose one over-arching question: *are we on track to fill each of our roles?* And they mean, *with good candidates?*

Recruiters will be sitting there attempting to understand what the numbers mean, whereas the stakeholders are understandably interested in the quality of the quantity. *Volume recruiters* just cannot get onto the same page. They will answer this, if pushed, by stating that their processes are designed to attract great talent and to discern the stronger from the weaker candidates through each of the stages that they set down. Other than that, they always respond in purely quantitative terms and hope that quality will be assumed as a *'given'.*

I have no wish to flog a dead horse on this point, but I think we all know that the reliance on 'the process' as a guarantor of quality is facile codswallop. Utter tripe. But amazingly, organisations still deign to make use of what RPOs and other agencies dare to describe as services. And it can only be because for the recruiting organisation, they are willing to accept the candidates who are ultimately squeezed out of the end of the process as being good enough for the purposes they have in mind.

Perhaps some stakeholders just realise that if you pay peanuts, you get monkeys. However, given time, even random monkeys and typewriters should eventually come up with something valid. How long do they actually need to achieve that?

As a candidate though, you need to be mindful that upon entering the top of one of these funnels, your progress will not be determined by your skills or your strength as a candidate. It might nevertheless be determined by your relative strengths in the different skills or competencies that are individually tested in the process that has been designed.

If you are good at verbal reasoning, you are able to learn some competency examples structured in accordance with STAR (Situation, Task, Action, Results), and the chances are you will do well in a surprisingly high number of recruitment processes if you are confident in performing during a group exercise.

Unfortunately, that may mean you have to forget some of your principles and take a step away from performing as you should, were there valid and reliable processes in place. It means you have to be prepared to *game the processes*. And that can be problematic if you misread the game and perform even worse than you would, had you relied upon your own qualities and accomplishments.

And that really does sum up the twisted and warped reality of this modern-day recruitment debacle.

§

Spare a thought though, for the occupational psychologists who work for these organisations, particularly those with *chartered* status. You can be sure that they go through intense periods of self-loathing because they are required to support the bizarre, batshit philosophies and process decisions that they know are contradictory and completely against what they stand for. These are the people who are constantly fighting against malpractice within recruitment organisations but who keep their sanity by gaining as much training or sales work with which to occupy themselves so that they are not forced into doing the unthinkable in so far as their professional status and obligations define it to be. The tenure of these individuals within such recruitment organisations is typically very limited because they are constantly on the lookout for in-house positions with companies that are developing and selling occupational psychology products. Escaping situations where they will not be required to compromise on professional ethics is a bonus to boot!

So, as a candidate, when you read the organisational blurb that accompanies any section on selection and recruitment, do not be fooled by the fact that there may be creditable credentials for those involved in the design of the process which you will be undertaking because in practice they will have gone along with it only because they had a gun held to their head. Or the processes may be sound but are put into practice in such a way that validity and reliability are impaired. Most of them are as disgusted with what gets churned out, indeed, as you as candidates would be, were you privy to some of those restricted areas of the *private sphere* (which recruiters are so keen to exclude you from). I will explore this in more depth when I consider the notion of *Private and Public* in recruitment contexts.

§

All of this should provide some useful context to this concept of the *funnel*. Let me just take you one further step into the absurd. So many senior figures in recruitment, particularly those fixated on 1990s advertising logic, do not get any of this at all. The wondrous proposition is that they do not understand the fallacies of their own shoddy processes because they are still supremely wedded to ideas that are even more delusionary.

I have sat in high-level meetings when *Mr Thick-as-Pigshit-Top-Director* banged on about the *'best-in-class job postings'* and inspiring creative that led to high-volume responses and how they absolutely and categorically equated to success. With a rejection rate at the pre-screen stage of up to 40% on some pipelines and ultimately positions unfilled.

Not just on another planet but in a different universe.

You couldn't make it up. But these cowboys are out there at an agency or RPO near you.

Not understanding the number one rule, in fact, *the only rule*. It is all about hitting the hiring requirement.

Yes. Mind-bending that these people actually run recruitment businesses and do not seem to understand that you really do have to fill the vacancies with good staff in order to lay claim to success. It doesn't matter how many people responded to the advertisement. Or how flashy your creative is. Or whether you have learned how to share links on Twitter. Or whether you play Golf.

So, while it is absolutely the case that you have to have applications at the top of the funnel, you have to hit a qualitatively sustainable hiring return.

The funnel has to work from top to bottom, all the way down.

Trebles for show, doubles for dough, as my father used to say. You have to hit the requirement.

12 – The Psycho Matrix

The moral, legal, and self-defeating maze of psychometric testing

As a wise man once said:

'Fast, good, cheap: pick any two'. (Anon)

But we clearly do have to avail ourselves of *something* that will help us to discern the wheat from the chaff.

Now, I personally have a fondness for the inclusion of psychometric tests in assessment processes. Not because I think they are a panacea for all the ills of the subjective recruiter. But because they at least add one or more layers of objectivity into a process. Added to this, they offer us a degree of comparability with benchmarks and other candidates.

What sits behind the design and construction of a psychometric test is undoubtedly a high level of scientific theory that has been operationalised by experts in applied science, almost certainly regulated by chartered psychologists. Some recruiting organisations will use them exactly for this purpose – to check that their candidates meet a standard level of ability across a range of skills.

That should be game, set and match. But no, it is not. What screws with that whole proposition is the incessant recruitment wank-a-thon that proceeds with reckless abandon from the moment that such tests are put in place.

Unfortunately, there is only so much that experts can do with a high-quality product before matters are taken out of their hands and used by people who, for want of a better expression, have not got the slightest inkling about what occurs.

You see, in the world of recruitment, the never-ending challenge is, as we noted in the last chapter, to attract a pool of good eggs and then whittle down the thousands who appear at the top of the funnel into a viable shortlist of candidates for assessment and then appointment.

It is therefore in the interest of recruiters to use the most cost-effective methods of screening when the applicant numbers are at their highest. Clearly, one of the ways in which to do this is in the use of automation. This is where psychometric tests have been plucked from their comfortable domain of scientific expertise and rather less comfortably plonked into the world of cost-effective operational tactics.

It is like lashing the caviar onto your corndog.

What this means in practice is that those who design operational processes use single psychometric tests as a way of bulk-screening candidates out of the whole process. This, I am afraid to say, is flawed to the extreme. As an aside, the *British Psychological Society (BPS)* recommends that candidates should not be screened out of application processes on the basis of single psychometric tests anyway[vi]. In the event that they are, the BPS states that it is essential that the criteria on which they are being screened out relate directly to the subject of the test – and that adequate performance in the test is an essential requirement of the role.

And this is where everything runs into difficulty.

§

For the BPS, the minimum standard of performance in a psychometric ability test would be achieving a score of at least the thirty-first percentile and above. Now this is not too controversial from their perspective because it is an acceptable level of quality performance below which a candidate might rightly be assumed to not have sufficient ability to perform effectively. Unfortunately, that is an argument that is grounded not only in common sense but also in scientific logic.

Therefore, it will not hold too much sway with the pragmatic concerns of recruiters, who simply need to fill positions and do so cost-effectively. You see, for the recruiters, it is about reducing high numbers to low numbers at a comparatively low cost. Accordingly, it is in their interest to run a test and then to set a pass mark at a relatively high level in order to remove swathes of the lower-performing candidates from the process at the earliest possible stage.

They will justify this by saying that this ensures that only the best candidates advance to the next stage of the process.

Now if you are a scientist or somebody who has a wider breadth of appreciation of recruitment processes than simply numbers, you will justly be aghast at this proposition. It has a number of serious implications.

Firstly, as the psychometric test will very often be assessing candidates on the basis of single dimensions, i.e. *verbal reasoning*, or *numerical reasoning*, it is something of a stretch to say that the individuals who perform the highest in these individual tests are necessarily going to be the strongest candidates overall. However, I have lost count of the times I have seen people enquiring about the predictive validity of a *verbal reasoning test (VRT)* when the final assessment centre has tested six different competencies. And not happy when it is explained that the *VRT* tests one dimension – and still not happy when offered alternatives with more breadth instead of a single *VRT*.

Mainly because of the cost. Ok, you will opt for *Discrimination Max*, then Madam?

So, in the simplest terms, unless the role itself is purely focused on verbal reasoning or numerical reasoning, this is not the best way to go to reduce the numbers. To cite a real-world example, it would be like suggesting that Ronaldo was a better footballer than Messi, simply because he performed better in a test of heading the ball. Such a test would of course completely ignore wider considerations of a range of football skills, such as shooting, dribbling, movement etc. But take it from me, your average recruiter will not take heed of this obvious discrepancy or shortfall in rationale. To your *funnel*-visioned and thick-as-dogshit recruiter, the highest-performing candidates in any given test will equate to the highest-performing candidates, full stop.

Yes, ladies and gentlemen, the situation is abysmal and, may I say, critical.

§

To develop the point further, which incorporates moral, legal, and pragmatic considerations, we have the level of *adverse impact* that such a use of these tests *in practice* might introduce into a recruitment process.

What I should make clear, is that adverse impact and the use of psychometric ability tests are two concepts that are well-known and acknowledged in recruitment circles. Yet despite this, the drive towards *diversity and inclusion* in organisations will be cast aside like a used tissue when the prospect of increased costs raises its ugly head. I should explain a little further.

Essentially, there is a considerable body of evidence that suggests that candidates from particular minority groups, specifically BAME, will tend to perform at a lower level on timed online psychometric ability tests. This is not to say that individuals from those backgrounds have a lower level of ability, but it is to say that the method of testing, i.e. an online timed test that is designed from a single and different cultural perspective, might introduce obstacles for such individuals that far exceed the challenges that other candidates will face.

While this has not been fully scientifically explained, it is likely that tests that reward candidates for a higher number of correct answers may significantly disadvantage candidates who need to think a lot more about questions that are couched in ways that are unfamiliar to them. For example, questions that are *specifically culturally located*, e.g. written from the perspective of a white middle-class man, may well use terminology and phrases that are often unfamiliar to individuals of other backgrounds, e.g. those who are not native speakers of English.

So, it is not a question of ability per se, it is about the format and the design of tests that may lead to candidates from different backgrounds scoring less highly. We might say that there is *potential* for adverse impact in these tests and that this can be exacerbated *depending on which target benchmark is used*.

This issue of adverse impact is typically measured by reviewing the performance scores of candidates within particular groups and then comparing those scores with those of the candidates from the highest-performing group.

So, for example, if *White British* candidates are the highest scoring group at a stage and their pass rate is 80%, it is expected that candidates from all other groups should have a pass rate of at least 64% (i.e. 80% of the pass rate of the highest scoring group). This is known as the 80/20 Rule which determines that the pass rate for all groups ought to remain within 20% of the highest-scoring group (usually *White British* candidates).

The difference in expectations can be explained inter alia by a number of factors such as test design (as discussed), the equality of social opportunity, and the context of the recruitment process. This final point is how candidates feel that the level of opportunity that they may have is important and often underestimated. It is about the context of the test and the candidate's application. Do they see the recruiting organisation as one which will give them a fair crack of the whip? These matters are important in helping candidates get off on the right foot. Naturally, there are as always, distributions of capability and performance that occur.

§

It is only when the differences exceed that 20% gap, that test administrators should acknowledge that the test itself has unwarrantedly contributed to a degree of disadvantage to that group that would be unacceptable in relation to the provision of equality for all candidates. It pushes the difference to a higher level that would otherwise occur as a result of the other factors combined.

Using a higher benchmark to eliminate more candidates at a test stage is a common cause of seeing that difference exceed 20%, sometimes by quite a distance. As the chosen point for the benchmark rises, the performance gap between groups of candidates is also likely to rise. Therefore, there is an increasingly greater likelihood that in such circumstances, a more pronounced degree of adverse impact will be introduced to the detriment of minority candidates.

Were recruiters to follow BPS guidelines and use the tests only to assess minimum capability for the role in question, it would be entirely justifiable even if it meant that the pass rate for minority candidates was still significantly lower than that of the highest-performing groups. That is because in this instance, the decision to benchmark at the 31st percentile can be justified entirely on the basis of quality. You could argue that it just happened to be the case that from this particular cohort of candidates, performance in one group was lower by chance.

Nobody would expect any organisation to reduce a standard below an acceptable level of performance under any circumstances.

Be that as it may, when you are applying an artificially higher benchmark, simply to reduce numbers to the suitable number that you require yourself at the next stage of the application process, you are achieving an undesirable by-product. You are increasing the likelihood of removing candidates from the process who will have demonstrated a standard of performance that was good enough for the job. Accordingly, these will fall below the benchmark, arguably as a result of the impact of a test administered in a way that was known to penalise members of particular groups at the higher percentiles.

Intuitively we know that this is neither a wise nor a fair approach. In legal terms, we are entering the realms of indirect discrimination on the grounds of race.

Now, owing to the tremendously complex nature of employment law, I will not deign to define what would constitute discrimination. Indeed, you might conclude that the paucity of precedent in some areas reflects the fiendishly difficult proposition in establishing a successful case. Suffice is to say that the Equality Act (2010) requires law-abiding citizens and bodies to use *proportionate means* to achieve *legitimate aims*[vii].

Demonstrating the *legitimate aim* of reducing a high number of applicants to a sufficiently manageable number in line with realistic hiring numbers will not prove too challenging for Rumpole, should he be so briefed. The tribunals will not even generally be too concerned at closely examining the tools that are chosen though m'learned friends will usually line up some sort of corroboration from the BPS or chartered psychologists. However, a tribunal judge will insist on hearing from them directly on the rare occasions that their expertise is required to be tested on a point. The key to it all, though, is in the proportionate application.

Is the use of a higher benchmark to whittle down the numbers disproportionate if high levels of adverse impact can be demonstrated in the cohort?

To date, it has not been successfully presented in court by a claimant but remains a spectre for all volume recruiters. If ever proven, the whole commercial case for many volume recruitment operations and contracts would be blown out of the water, overnight. Completely torpedoed.

But you would hope, on the basis that something is clearly not morally sound here, that recruiters would already be seeking alternatives, without having to be forced to do it by the rule of law?

On that very basis alone, you would like to think that organisations would not use these tests in such a way. What makes it even worse, is that in deciding the cut-off scores, these are done with the full knowledge of individual candidate backgrounds, so recruiters will always know that setting scores at particularly high levels will in practice have a potentially greater level of adverse impact on candidates from certain backgrounds.

But no, there is not the slightest appetite to change tack. It is quite simply the darkest of recruitment practices currently in place today.

For all their blog postings and *thought leadership* on the importance and criticality of diversity and inclusion, recruiters by these very actions and who use this approach of elevated benchmarks are likely to be trampling over the hopes and aspirations of whole groups within the cohorts they test. Prioritising cash savings to limit the number of candidates who move forward through to the latter stages of recruitment processes. It is the height of hypocrisy.

And of course, in not following BPS guidance in the first instance, the guidance of experts, a whole host of other good-enough candidates bite the dust.

§

The greatest irony of this is that there are even more cost-effective ways of distinguishing between stronger and weaker candidates that can be achieved as long as organisations are willing to put down some up-front investment. An example of this might be to construct a *Situational Judgement Test (SJT)* that is designed and later validated to eliminate potential issues for candidates. Designers might make that language as neutral as possible, and these tests can be structured to examine key elements of the role across a number of behaviours or competencies. This would add a suitable range of dimensions for testing that could be better justified as grounds for progressing a candidate or rejecting them from a process and can be untimed so that candidates who need more time to digest particular turns of phrase, would not be unduly penalised.

Now designing and validating an *SJT* is probably not going to leave you with much change out of £20k. But when you consider that processing 1,000 candidates through an online test at one single stage is going to cost you between £3k and £20k (depending on the test and the volume deal that you may have from your supplier), even on a financial basis, that investment is going to very quickly pay for itself in any volume recruitment exercise. It would just be a matter of convincing your average everyday psychotic finance director of firstly the need to invest once in a while when there is not an immediate return on the same month's balance sheet, or maybe just to do the right thing.

Do not hold your breath on either count.

The only reason that recruitment companies have got away with this for so long is that the test for discrimination (direct or indirect) is stringent and it is not a given to convince a tribunal that discrimination has occurred simply because potentially discriminatory actions have been taken. And that is all the wriggle-room that the recruitment worms need in order to be able to carry on with their potentially discriminatory and plainly unscientific approaches.

But you should not be too surprised that this type of thing happens. As I have said before and will doubtlessly repeat over the course of this book, it is not about getting the best talent. It is neither about doing what is morally right, nor right for competitive advantage nor for organisations where you are the supplier recruiter.

It is a numbers game, where positions are filled with people who are good enough to do the job and where fees are paid accordingly.

That is it. That is recruitment.

§

Unfortunately, anybody who can put the most cogent of arguments forward is unlikely to change the way things are done. The only hope that people have is that individual stakeholders involved in the processes of recruitment stand up and put into practice the essence of what they are tirelessly and almost obsessively keen to wedge into their bullshit *thought leadership* blogs.

But please refrain from being overly optimistic on this score. It is nonetheless commendable, in bad taste terms, that these recruiters can keep a straight face and continue to harp on about quality *thought leadership* and *best practice* when they so blatantly ignore not only what is common sense and science but the guidance given from industry and professional experts. The very same experts whom they are otherwise very keen to quote in their web content and proposals that they submit to their clients.

It is barefaced hypocrisy of the highest order but now part-and-parcel of the organic character reference for recruitment practitioners.

§

It is also the case that the operational steps taken when using tests in practice can lead to further problems for candidates. As these tests are taken off the shelf from psychometric test providers, they are an attractive proposition for the recruiter who will not need to spend excessive amounts of man-hours administering the process.

All they will need to do is load in the names of the candidates who will be invited to the test, and the test platform will ensure that the test is emailed out directly to candidates or will provide test links to the operational teams in whatever company to send out themselves. If the company then gives the candidates, let us say, one week to complete the test, the only further work that the organisation will need to do, except for re-set tests or deal with candidate queries, will be to collect the results at the end of the test period.

Now you would not think that recruiters could balls that one up. Something that was carefully designed, with clearly established processes. But you would be wrong. For a start, it is the norm rather than the exception that candidates will be missed off invitation lists altogether in volume processes.

It is also another common feature of the administration of these tests that candidates who request reasonable adjustments will either not get them at all or will receive an incorrect adjustment that leaves them still at a disadvantage in relation to other candidates. And when you, as candidates, complain that you have been, ahem, withdrawn for non-completion of your tests, there will be very little that you can do about it. After all, people generally do not like admitting to their mistakes, and with a fast-moving recruitment timeline, it is often too late to put people back into a recruitment process when subsequent stages have passed.

Therefore, the path of least resistance is frequently taken to deny any error on the part of the recruitment organisation. The issue with volume recruitment is that this is the type of activity that is typically outsourced to external providers, who are best placed from a perspective of resource and uneven distribution of work, to handle campaigns on behalf of blue-chip organisations.

That spells even worse news for candidates because these organisations have a vested interest in protecting their relationships with their clients and are protected by a reasonably impermeable layer of bureaucracy that prevents any meaningful investigation of their activities. Their very special *private sub-sphere*, which we go on to discuss in a later chapter, makes this possible.

Ultimately, without clear evidence to the contrary, recruiting organisations — clients if you like, in such an outsourcing scenario — will take the word of their supplier over their candidates with very few exceptions. There are complex combinations of thoughts that drive this approach, which involve, for example, a recruiter's desire to opt for the easiest path.

Their thoughts are further stimulated by a fear that any such errors will start to raise questions in the minds of more senior stakeholders and create more work for their subordinates, who will then need to demonstrate that they are monitoring supplier performance more effectively.

It may also bring into question the judgement of those who brought in those suppliers in the first instance, but the main consideration will always be that people will want to avoid additional work, which can of course be avoided by a firm denial to a candidate who, frankly, has little power in a structure and process that is defined and controlled by recruiter.

It is a nauseating thought that opportunities can hinge on the incompetence and dishonesty of recruiters. But thousands of candidates every year lose out for precisely these kinds of reasons. And they have absolutely no redress even if the subterfuge is discovered. Once again, the reason for this is that remedies in courts and tribunals can only be sought under very specific areas. Rectifying cockups is not one of them.

If psychometrics and other online tests veer into view, make sure that you are on point and vigilant.

The chances are that nobody else will be.

13 – The New Black

The concepts of Diversity and Inclusion on recruitment agendas

Diversity and Inclusion or *D&I*, are two conceptual elements that have been deftly fused together and have become one of the organisational buzz phrases of the early twenty-first century. CEOs and other high-flying figures cannot contain themselves and will routinely blunderbuss the term at audiences, or for that matter, anybody who will stop for five minutes and listen.

But because people in these exalted positions hop onto bandwagons in the search for revenue, without ever truly understanding what the terms mean, we should undertake some unpacking of the term in order to understand what it means and how things play out in practice.

Generally speaking, the lucre-crazed executives who are looking to open whatever markets they can blandly talk about just *diversity*. In their minds, diversity is an all-encompassing piece of terminology that reflects the fact that their own organisation welcomes individuals from different ethnic backgrounds – those with disabilities or different sexual preferences, to name but a few.

This is for several reasons.

As they trawl through the Internet to find out more about the very industries in which their own organisations are involved, they will read a lot about organisations reporting on diversity statistics. So, in the finest tradition of *concept appropriation*, these executives lift and drop the term *diversity* and weld it into their own policies and service offerings. What they do not realise, is that when those who are truly in the know refer to diversity, they are using the term *descriptively* to signal the degree of difference within their organisations.

It is a term used to describe status at any point in time. Furthermore, because they tend to focus on specific areas of difference, namely diversity and disability, our favourite thick-as-plank executives in recruitment circles assume that these are the only categories that matter when seeking to attain *difference*. They are also mindful of the fact that there would be a legal requirement to offer equality of opportunity, in so far as those with protected characteristics are concerned.

But that of course only scratches the surface of what leading organisations perceive as constituting diversity. And this is where it gets tricky because these leading organisations are promoting diversity from a moral perspective as well as one that makes business sense rather than simply doing something in order to suck in some wonga and of course, to avoid being hiked up in front of M'Lud.

Conscientious organisations go much further than simply ensuring that there is equal opportunity for all in terms of applications for vacancies. They do not simply look to increase the number of applications from particular groups but are particularly diligent in ensuring that the representation of these groups is maintained throughout the recruitment process. Over and above this – and this is the whole point of this subject matter being relevant at all – they ensure that the diverse workforce is equally *inclusive* for all.

And that is the piece that recruitment agencies do not and cannot grasp. The reason for this is that recruiters, simply because they have to do it, have it on their agenda to track the prevalence of specific diversity characteristics during their processes. However, they rarely demonstrate the behaviours that reflect that diversity is embraced in their processes.

The recruiters I have encountered would absolutely ensure that advertisements were posted where high numbers of minority candidates, for example, would apply. But then, after having received high volumes of applications, they would not baulk at applying artificially higher test benchmarks in order to reduce the numbers of applicants as the process progressed through the funnel. In that type of situation, the net result is frequently that very few candidates from BAME backgrounds would progress to the latter stages. Also, very little – if any – activity to promote engagement with members of these groups would take place as the processes moved forward.

They would just be *the 6 BAMEs*, a categorised total.

§

So, from that perspective, we are talking about lip service to diversity and a side-step for inclusivity because the recruitment processes are designed for reasons of commercial advantage to be disproportionately exclusive. What is more, should candidates ever decide to raise a grievance in relation to the presence or the potential presence of adverse impact in testing stages, they will receive short shrift.

Recruiters rely on the fact that the stress and effort, not to mention the cost, will see off all but the most determined of litigants.

And while it may sound shocking to hear, sifts are generally not *blind*, that is to say, names and places of birth, along with other indicators of personal characteristics, are evident to the person performing the sift. Candidates with names that suggest a Middle Eastern or African background will be subject to rigorous checking, you mark my words, particularly on their educational qualifications. It would not be unheard of for African candidates to be disproportionately represented at a qualification check stage, to the point where they may not progress any further owing to an absence of absolute verification.

This may also be the case even if on paper their qualifications are deemed to meet the minimum criteria because there will likely be more of a focus on whether the documents presented are genuine or fraudulent. With West African candidates in particular, the presumption will always be that the documents should be treated with suspicion unless proven otherwise. Of course, none of this ever floats to the surface, for obvious reasons.

§

Now there are other aspects of diversity and inclusion that are worth looking at within the context of recruitment. I have written extensively on exactly this subject over the years, helping businesses and site owners keen to keep their *thought leadership* blogs pumping. Naturally, when pushing this kind of content out, you are always keen to understand how it is received and the contribution it is making to the wider debates.

These would moreover be original pieces and not just some articles that would be found via a search engine and regurgitated. The pieces were duly published, minus any name credit (for that is often the name of the game when you are in the writing sphere) and are, believe it or not, still out there for the perusal of the populace. Some refreshingly unique analyses on the subjects of reasonable adjustments, autistic spectrum disorders and ethnicity.

Well on the adjustments piece, only two types of feedback emerged. Firstly, the quantitative. They had ranked as the highest 'clicked' articles on the blog – I think one was viewed 47 times in the first week. This was fed back to me as 'awesome'. Not sure why, but hey, let us not stare into the choppers of the proverbial mare. The second was qualitative. Some of the people who reported back had said that they were a great read but clearly (by virtue of their follow-up questions) had not understood the content.

This raised a couple of questions about people involved in recruiting processes, *thought leadership*, how *diversity* and *inclusion* were being viewed and the essence of the whole darned shooting match. But firstly, let me say a few words about the articles themselves, which will help to illustrate my points.

I should first state that in terms of D&I, disabled candidates have certainly fared a lot better in recruitment because recruiters have started to get their heads around the concept of reasonable adjustments. But it is by no means unflawed – would you honestly expect a shit-kicking, corner-cutting industry to do any different?

Candidates who request adjustments for physical disabilities are likely to see responsive recruiters, and this is as much about their awareness of compliance elsewhere in everyday life, where they see that shops, for example, have almost universally adjusted access to their premises. This is high-profile and visible every day. People in recruitment are therefore aware that these are matters to which they too must attend or likely face adverse publicity and sanctions.

So, my first article looked at the question of *reasonable adjustments (RAs)* in practice.

I kicked off with a pretty standard explanation of the legal requirements to consider *RAs* and the reasons why it is a focus for attention – legal requirements, morality, the practical advantages of skills and knowledge attainment for any organisation that promotes diversity and inclusivity thereof. Nothing too controversial there though I did hint that for some organisations, there is a bonus of feelgood and some self-congratulatory celebrations. It is always nice to be seen to be nice, as they say.

I then made the point that while it all made sense, businesses are looking to do it primarily because they have to and that this is betrayed in the language they use.

I drove the point home by highlighting the universal practice of using the precise term *'reasonable adjustment'* directly in interactions with job applicants and employees. It struck me (and still does) as somewhat bizarre like providing a service before the customers had even been asked what they wanted. The reasonable adjustment is after all the final product. Or rather the *adjustment* is, with the *reasonable* standing as a modifier to signify that the provider of the adjustment had agreed that it could stand.

But recruiters steam on in with the notion of *reasonable adjustments*, in what sounds to an onlooker (and likely a candidate) as their opening salvo in what is pitched to be a battle.

There are two points here. Recruiters are aware of the legal concept of *RAs* and want an efficient 'route 1' response. After all, we are frequently advised, in the spirit of efficiency and results, to *'start with the end goal in mind'*. This does nevertheless avoid the process of discovery, in favour of, well, an operational process. *'Let us just find out what they want and give it to them'.*

The second point is that organisations, not just recruiters, love to fall back on labels and categorisations. These help everyone to work efficiently and avoid repetition and confusion through implied meaning.

Does somebody want reasonable adjustments? Ok, add them to the list, and we'll call them and offer our standard provisions. At the same time, we are putting *RA* candidates into a pot that is only marginally more helpful than having one large pot of all candidates. This is one area, where at the point that we engage with candidates, the label should stand as purely an indicator that something different needs to happen.

What that 'something' is will be determined by a discussion that needs to happen several steps back.

§

The language that actually tends to be used comes straight from the statute, which is then just lifted and shifted into processes and interactions. At this stage, it is not examined and applied to a real person or circumstances, but it does nevertheless serve a purpose. It suggests that recruiters and employers are cementing an unequivocal connection between action and legal obligation. Recruiters are being crystal clear that they are meeting their legal obligations.

And to candidates, it jars.

This language speaks volumes about how adjustments are viewed and about motivations to act. You might argue with some credence that it is the preoccupation with *diversity* being the (current) holiest of Holy Grail outcomes that have made this less about an equalisation of opportunity and more about a box to be ticked.

My overarching comment was that everything should start with the individual and what they needed. In focusing on *reasonable adjustments* and not on *individual needs*, organisations are actually starting in the wrong place.

It then makes everything truly candidate-centric and embraces not only the notion of equal opportunity but more crucially that of *inclusion.*

You would hope that organisations had as their primary goal as businesses to enrich their products and services by attracting great talent. And the great part about the shift to individual needs is that these might not relate to protected characteristics. By including any candidates who are not protected and meeting their individual needs, you will be embracing a wider definition of D&I and similarly wider achievement (and success) for your organisation.

And of course, avoiding situations where reasonable adjustments as a starting point fail to hit the mark by failing to get to the heart of the *need.*

In not doing all of this, we are left with a different kind of diversity. Something one-dimensional to the demographic with very little change to the breadth or the depth of an organisation's footprint.

All this labelling is an indicator of a mindset and of a focus on the buzzwords and terms rather than the essence of a sound and fundamentally grounded methodology.

All sensible stuff. Not necessarily ground-breaking because there are already recruiting organisations out there who have long since adopted the language and the mindset of the individual need. Nevertheless, pithy analysis of an existing issue in recruitment that had been, for the large part, unresolved.

But you know, the people who actually read it, as far as we know, just didn't get it. Their feedback was largely about whether the author was suggesting a change in the use of terminology. They didn't realise that it was not just a question of changing words but of changing hearts and minds. And it was going to involve more time spent on a comparatively small percentage of candidates.

And that, my friends, meant that there was not the slightest motivation to engage. Hearts and minds in recruitment? More time spent but no extra billings? You have got to be *having a larf*.

§

Unsurprisingly, my piece on ASDs and the autistic spectrum didn't fare much better, either. Most of the people who came back on that one were talking about what organisations might do to adjust bright lights in the office.

It seemed as if the first reaction of the reading public had been to pump 'autism' into *a* search engine. But that is exactly what we all have to contend with in the world of recruitment. We could have substituted *Autism* and *ASD* with *Judaism* and *Jews* and probably received some queries about skullcaps.

They just do not do the detail at all.

I talked about the stigmatisation, but even less popularly I talked not only about adjustments but also alternative testing and the endemic issue of asking for RAs for candidates within application forms, and I made it clear that some candidates will want adjustments to be made so that they can have an alternative application process.

All viable points, which, as many of you will know, were supported in law at tribunal (Brookes, 2017)[viii].

In calling for the transformation of organisations rather than opting for the warmth of those who reassure us with their echo of our comfortable, tried-and-tested customs and practices, I realised that I had overstretched. In spite of the Brookes case, with its £860 compensation, the vast majority of recruiters who do not give the slightest of tosses anyway are hardly going to be whipped into a sense of righteousness at the prospect of ultimately having to pay out a small percentage of the cost of setting up alternative assessment in the future. And if you think that reputation matters, how many people can even remember the parties involved in tribunal cases?

Do you really believe that a recruiter will pay out £10k in order to facilitate alternative assessments that help them avoid forking out £1k down the line? They would rather just pass the candidates through if they had to. You see, those engaged in recruitment will, with some notable exceptions, not want any more adjustments on the radar than those that are forced onto them by the rule of law.

But more than the issue itself, the world of recruiting loves the views and opinions on supporting D&I. They love the analysis and recommendations. They will read, consume, and share them.

But will they change in practice? Very few will because in practice everything is measured on the single dimension of pounds, shillings, and pence.

My piece on ethnicity garnered nothing. Maybe it was not actually a great piece. After all, sometimes the very best writers produce articles that bomb. Perhaps it just reflected that ethnicity is no longer as hip as it once was in recruitment circles. Very few do actually seem all that motivated to address any related challenges unless they have a large stick or carrot waved in their direction.

I was nonetheless grateful to those who did post my articles. The exposure was ultimately great for (my) business.

§

Well, when all is said and done, and in spite of the best intentions from many of those involved in recruitment, the provision of reasonable adjustments is still largely seen as an afterthought and a bit of a hassle. Even organisations that run *Two Ticks* or *Disability Confident* schemes (you may also be familiar with the *Guaranteed Interview Scheme* as an alternative moniker) demonstrate that they are often incompetent in getting these schemes effectively operational. On many occasions, I have seen these businesses struggle to squeeze disabled candidates into assessment events with recruiters citing 'a lack of availability'.

Yet the correct process for a *Disability Confident* scheme stipulates that those candidates meeting the minimum criteria and the standard for each test should be offered the first places at the final interview – before all others. This means that any variable benchmark to determine the remaining attendees should be finalised only when the candidates applying under *Two Ticks* or a similar scheme have been confirmed and booked in.

So often in practice, hardly inclusive and not foreshadowing inclusion once in role. Not to mention incorrect procedurally.

Show me an adherent to that process, and I will not show you an agency or an RPO.

§

So, my message to candidates who might be affected by recruitment organisations' lack of awareness of *inclusion* would be this. If you need reasonable adjustments, make sure these are noted in the appropriate place on the application form, but always send a separate communication that is read-receipted. Do not trust the organisation to have an applicable process that will draw all the adjustment information out for action. Frequently, it gets completely overlooked.

Furthermore, as you progress through the process, ensure that you are again making further contact with the recruitment teams because it may be that additional adjustments are required, depending on the nature of what is being tested. If in any doubt, you should enquire about the details of the process and the format of tests that are going to be undertaken. Only then can you ensure that the right adjustments are put in place.

The reason why this is so important and why action is required at the earliest possible point, I will go into much more detail shortly. This is particularly important when dealing with RPOs, so more on that later. It is also essential, should you be rejected from the process and you are applying as part of a *Disability Confident* scheme, that you request detailed feedback that outlines the standard benchmark (this is the one that would apply to you), the variable benchmark (this was the score that would apply to all other candidates who had *not* declared disability and were *not* applying as part of the scheme) as well as your own score.

Do not be surprised when you ask for this information for there to be a pause in communications and for you to receive a subsequent invitation to the next stage. I cannot think of any disabled candidate who has not experienced that reversal of good fortune at some stage during their job-seeking career! It is always worth being tenacious on this point so that you do not lose out by reason of indifference from others.

My advice to candidates from minority ethnic backgrounds would be to focus on other areas, namely the processes themselves and how they are delivered. Absolutely raise the question of *blind sifting*, citing the *UK Civil Service* as a leading force in making this approach to assessment as standard, following a Cabinet Office directive from David Cameron in November 2015. Certainly, raise a question mark over any timed ability tests, at the very least to put them on notice that you are on the case about factors on which your application may firmly rest. This may stimulate some internal discussion – rest assured, your average *recruitment advisor* will hoof this over to their line manager or the hiring manager with the ferocity of a Federer forehand. Way above their pay grade because it reeks of complaint accelerant, so to speak.

This might make the process administrators a tad more wary about adopting a relatively high benchmark in order to reduce the numbers passing through. Once again, it is not a question of members of these groups having a lower level of ability, but it is a concern when the scores are set at a high level that BAME candidates may be needlessly rejected even though they demonstrate sufficient skills to do the job.

The problem with recruitment companies is that passing more candidates through each stage raises their costs. And if it is a choice between higher costs and lower BAME representation, you can bet your bottom Euro that they will opt for the latter. Let us be quite clear on the reasons for this. Quite simply, the notion of inclusion carries very little importance to recruiters as long as they can maintain an impressive client list and a corresponding high level of access to the maximum number of revenue streams.

As far as recruitment companies and RPOs are concerned, whatever tosh you read on their websites about the promotion of *Diversity and Inclusion*, take it with a pinch of salt. That is not to say there is no positive activity going on, but much of this is done simply because people are watching over their shoulders and because they see it as useful new business collateral.

They would otherwise not have any incentive to promote D&I because doing so involves more expense in the administration of processes, which they will of course not see as an investment. Agencies and RPOs recruit hires for other organisations, so once the individuals are hired, they are handed off. Any additional activity that smooths the way forward into the hiring organisation,? Don't make me laugh. It pushes up costs and squeezes margin. The only way that idea gets to the table is if a hiring manager funds it. Otherwise, it doesn't make it into first gear, full stop.

§

In brief – whatever the background or personal characteristics of candidates, the fees will be the same. Morality and forward-thinking decisions that bring tangible benefits down the line do not feature. It is all about the immediate balance sheets.

Looking at a wider interpretation of D&I, if you are a candidate who has other (unprotected) characteristics that you feel make you different, then what I am about to tell you will not fill you with the greatest of confidence. Issues around gender, and even to a degree sexuality, and certainly introversion, ginger hair or birthmarks are likely to see you as the object of the gossip mill propagated by the little boys' clubs that predominate in recruitment agencies and RPOs. You will even see some good old-fashioned 1920s misogyny if the circumstances are right. It is at epidemic proportions. In fact, it is an epidemic, spread through the almost federalist cliques that form when people move from organisation to organisation in the world of recruitment.

The best advice I can give is that, as much as possible, you should anticipate the challenges that you might encounter and ensure that you are well-equipped in terms of processes and procedures to follow in order to gain redress.

In spite of suggestions that we have become a more liberal society, there remain strong prejudicial undercurrents in all these companies which are driven by *halo and horns* idealistic visions of what '*good*' looks like. It is a deeply regressive culture and sadly measures need to be taken in order for candidates to protect themselves. While you will not have much support in your attempts to unpick any problems, you will at least be prepared and able to manage your concerns effectively.

You see, half of these people are not even aware that what they are doing is wrong or at least cannot see where right and wrong are demarked. They are also not used to being challenged.

Therefore, you do have a fighting chance of their egos working in your favour, particularly if you give them enough rope. It is not unheard of for them to create worse problems for themselves through their subsequent actions or responses to the complaints they receive. Use everything you can to influence action.

So, on the subject of knuckle-dragging Neanderthals, this leads me nicely onto one of my favourite subjects: the world of *Recruitment Process Outsourcing* or *RPO*.

We are about to hit new lows.

14 – All Play and No Work Makes Jack

The very special role of Volume RPOs

For those of you who are familiar with my previous book, *Flypaper for Freaks* – in which I investigated the *odious world of outsourced contact centres* – you will know that I have *just a few* issues with the compatibility of mainstream volume delivery principles and the notion of service provision. Or at least, with the balance that is routinely applied between these in practice.

Now the world of volume recruitment brings forth a different area of activity for us to consider in the world of recruitment. It is a domain where some of the least favourable aspects of modern commercial life converge to formulate enterprises that are unscrupulous in their race to the bottom.

If you read *Flypaper*, you are probably going to guess what horror awaits. Not only do you have these unfeasibly twisted and unprincipled recruiters at work, but some of them have turned to volume delivery as their area of operation and in doing so have joined forces with the worst of the worst from the contact centre world. Yes, Ladies and Gentlemen, welcome to the world of *Recruitment Process Outsourcing* or *RPO*. Were Philip Larkin[ix] alive, he would have completely rewritten his poem and turned his attention to RPOs.

It would not be your Mum and Dad who do what they do. It would be the RPO shit-machine.

Clients and candidates alike, nobody is spared from the spray.

It does not mean that all volume recruitment exercises are outsourced but most of the high-volume stuff is. It is a question of seasonality, the distribution of work and the process element that gives organisations a financial incentive to outsource – bolstered by the increased confidence – that it is largely about processes. The RPOs also cite expertise, but it is debatable whether organisations really do swallow that.

So, what could possibly go wrong?

Actually, everything but hey, let us run with it for a moment.

Just take a minute to think about what it is like when you get ripped off. Then, imagine the immense frustration of dealing with an incompetent. None of that is going to be pleasant. But if you combine it all in a blender, give it a good whisk and serve it up, you have the taste of RPO. It is the most unpleasant concoction of charlatans, fraud, theft, incompetence, dishonesty, and sub-sociopathic lunacy.

And do you know what, I think I have just understated that. But let me tell you why my reference for the RPO world is hardly glowing.

§

You see as a starting point, RPOs are outsourcing organisations, so they need to sell the benefits of their products and services to prospective clients. So of course, the marketing teams and frankly every other person in a position of authority are straining to puff up the credentials of the organisation, and they present a picture to the world that suggests that the RPO is a credible player in whatever markets they choose to involve themselves.

Now you know what's coming.

All the usual *thought leadership* blogs, awards entries, conferences, and case studies.

Even before we deign to dive into the ocean of deplorable faux pas that account for 70% of the RPO world's surface, just consider the prospect of your application reaching a crucial stage in the process during a notable calendar event – like *Hallowe'en*, *Comic Relief*, or *Children in Need*, to name but a few.

Instead of verifying your test results or sending you that invitation to interview that you desperately need to plan, there is a high chance that this will have been shelved in preference to a game of crazy golf, *guessing the identity of the baby* or even the themed decoration of the team pods.

It is the sort of cheap motivational strategy in call centres that went sour in the mid-1990s. But to the self-important, low-rent upstarts who crawl all over RPO delivery with their Web-searched professional knowledge at the pinnacle of these useless clown clusters, you, the candidate, will take a very distant second place.

And before you think that this seems like a buzz-killing attitude from an old fart, let me tell you that these organisations will think nothing of closing down their centres for a half-day in order to let the staff go home to get ready for an office party because they have read online that this stuff works and absolves them of all their previous sins. And the *Account Managers* in these companies have to get on the phone with the clients to communicate that all to them. It must look like the brass neck of, well, something very brass-necked.

The only redeeming factor in all of this is that relationship managers in RPOs are probably the biggest clowns in the clown compendium.

And the irony of all this? Staff turnover is still universally high in these factories, and the employees *detest* the management teams. But yet again, the candidates in the processes lose out.

As an example, a lot of RPOs manage seasonal work for their clients, like annual graduate campaigns. It makes sense for client companies, owing to the sharp spike in activity and the need to be able to turn on some instant support that can then be turned off during the periods when the work is not there. I can absolutely see the quantitative logic.

The problems however arise with the qualitative assessments.

In year two, managers and staff move on and are replaced by new people. So, the clients pay for a year one service in year two. Even if the same staff work on the campaign in the following year, they have only done it themselves once before. Once the previous campaign is over, they may not continue to embed themselves in the work or culture of their client until the next campaign revs up, particularly if the client contract is graduates-only.

So, you can end up with having a 10-year contract on paper, yet every year the quality of service is like they are doing it for the first time. Because many of them are. And before you think that these RPOs run sophisticated knowledge bases in the background, they do not. That would involve investment, with no corresponding return on the balance sheet.

It would be a non-starter. You would be shot for having the temerity to even think it, let alone say it. I have seen people disappear from organisational life for making far less radical suggestions.

We are talking about recruitment fast food. On the griddle, wrapped, purchased, and consumed. And tomorrow, you do not dwell on what you have had, and you do not really go around publicising where you go to dine.

When a staff member leaves, their knowledge and learning go with them straight out of the door. Training will often be a thirty-minute briefing and then they are off. No matter how glossy the slide decks and the marketing collateral, the reality is that we are talking low-cost volume production lines.

The hidden truths of RPO, if truly considered by clients who care about their brands, would drive a wholesale re-evaluation of their recruitment and resourcing strategies. And, I firmly believe, a contract exodus.

I could give examples of other things they do, but frankly I would probably lose the will to live. If you do get a chance to have a look at the sections in *Flypaper for Freaks*, on all of these themes covering the batshit management epic fails, you will get a little more insight into what I mean. In this respect, *RPOs* mirror *BPOs* and vice versa.

But to put not too fine a point on it, there is an unfeasibly large amount of hot air, designed to pump up the reputation and standing of RPOs that has absolutely no foundation in fact whatsoever. Just as an example, the vast majority of blogs that get published, simply as a result of a cursory scrape of the Internet with links published and no proprietary insight, are subjects that are massively misunderstood or out of context.

It is cringe comedy for the onlookers, but man, the RPO bods themselves, they think they are the bees' knees. Like their shit doesn't stink.

And let us not forget that these charlatans are operating in the world of recruitment. So, they are effectively gold-medal bullshitting about a process that itself is worthy of gold-medal bullshit. I mean it is not even like a restauranteur talking up a crap restaurant. He might lie, or blag a little, but at least the restaurant is a restaurant, doing what a restaurant should, albeit badly.

RPOs peddle their whoppers on a service that doesn't actually exist.

This is, as I may have mentioned in passing because *agency recruiters* generally do not recruit in the sense of what we all understand recruitment to be. They purport to be something but are actually in the business of doing something very different.

RPOs promise objective process-driven hiring that attracts and selects the very best talent. Well, such a service cannot possibly exist because it is a contradiction in terms.

So, you can see why RPOs occupy a very special place in the hearts and minds of people who are aghast at the immorality of the recruitment sphere. They are truly odious even if we decide to focus just on their lack of substance.

§

But then, there is an additional layer of knavery that takes this to a new level or, rather, a new depth. In order to deliver all the processes and procedures supporting the management of candidates in a recruitment process, RPOs need to enlist the support of contact centre experts and staff. And lo and behold, the world of *Business Process Outsourcing* has become a fertile recruiting ground for the RPO delivery teams. And we really shouldn't be surprised at this. In a world overwhelmingly dominated by *halo and horns*, if you are about to deliver products and services premised on fraud and deceit, and you need somebody to set up a delivery mechanism, the *BPO* contact centres would be your first port of call.

And that is why, when swathes of candidates are being processed through assessment stages, so many are at risk of being forgotten, misprocessed, or even deleted, and along with it seeing their hopes and opportunities crushed. You see while contact centre staff generally do not give two tosses about the outcomes and implications of what they do on a daily basis, you might argue that for the majority of tasks undertaken by them, those implications are likely to result in feelings of dissatisfaction or moments of inconvenience for customers. And they are usually errors that can be rectified if they are uncovered. Now I am not belittling these implications because in some instances this may result in fraud and the loss of money or reputation, for the victims concerned.

But with RPO processes and procedures, we are talking about something different. The processes are invariably more complex and are intrinsically connected to the legal rights of individuals and the very essence of their subsistence. The errors that frequently occur will relate to among other things, discriminatory acts and serious data breaches relating to sensitive and personal information. All of this rolls up into the denial of progress relating to job opportunities that people have earned through extensive and expensive periods of study.

In *volume RPO*s, you see it all. Random emails, incorrect rejections, job offers to the wrong candidates, personal data leaked, and candidates invited to assessments on the wrong dates. You name the procedural dropped balls and they are dropping as you read.

RPO chicanery tramples over rights, obligations, and progress. Candidates are rarely aware that it has even happened.

One of the principal reasons for this is that with outsourcing everything moves into a different dimension. In the RPO world, there is a *volume jungle*. Candidate applications go in and hires come out. But what happens in the jungle, nobody ever gets to understand. And should anybody decide to start to investigate, there is so much detail and variability that anything can be spun in any direction that the RPO chooses.

And in the course of my investigations, I have uncovered some examples of misconduct that would make your hair stand on end. It is truly shocking what some of these RPO organisations get away with. One of the reasons they do get away with things is, again connected with the reasons that *BPO* contact centre organisations can sail so close to the wind with such high levels of impunity. It is because clients do not wish to be held responsible for a lack of judgement that comes to pass as a result of RPO misconduct.

What I would say though, is that *RPO* clients are not complicit in the delivery of a shocking service in the same way that *BPO* clients are. And the primary reason for that is of course that the recruitment of high-quality staff is essential to the continued survival of their own organisations. Whereas *BPOs* do not give a damn about their customers, *RPO* clients absolutely care about the people who will be joining them at their side, in delivering the work of their organisation.

If I told you that you may have applied for a job, where all your personal and sensitive data had been sent to another client in error, would you be concerned?

If I told you that you had passed an assessment event for a highly competitive position, and an administrative error had miscounted your final score so that you were not offered a position, would you be concerned?

If I told you that an RPO had run a recruitment campaign for a critical public sector service, but had in error passed 400 failed candidates (and necessarily had rejected a further 400 others who had actually met the pass mark) due to the wrong answer key being loaded into a test – and then kept it covered up – would you be concerned?

I would be. In every one of these circumstances. But these are daily occurrences in RPO world. Yet to candidates, you wouldn't be any the wiser. And yet when these matters do float to the surface, the RPOs concerned will throw into the ring all manner of spun arguments, however unfeasible in order to muddy the waters. Sometimes these cock-ups are leaked to the press, but usually they remain well-hidden, particularly from the client organisations concerned.

§

One contact in the RPO world once told me that there was a formula for addressing service complaints from clients in order to deflect and defuse any concerns raised.

It went something like this:

- *'We do not exactly know what happened, but we think it was this'.*

(Translation: we know we messed up massively. But if we tell you what we found, it will open up other large cans of worms. So, we'll keep it vague and take a general kicking rather than have to get into specifics that might end up with us getting the chop. NB. 'This' will always be external to the company and something the company has no control over).

- *'(On any specific point), we can find no evidence that this happened/this is inconsistent with our account/findings'.*

(Translation: we know we did it, but we also know you cannot prove it).

- *'We will provide training and support and/or take internal action to address this'.*

(Translation: we will not actually do anything and because of data protection responsibilities, we will not be able to specify names or actions taken. But this line should be enough for you to put on the record that we are doing something, so it can be put to bed)

- *'We cannot find any record/evidence of that happening'.*

(Translation – we didn't find anything because we didn't look in the first place).

- *'We are sorry that the service fell short on this occasion/did not match what we aim to deliver'.*

(Translation – we are sorry that you were able to pin us down, so we can no longer deny our incompetence).

- *'Let us take a step back and look into this in more detail'.*

(Translation – if we stretch the post-mortem out for long enough, it will feel less raw, and people may leave on both sides, so the problem/anger about the problem will start to fade, and it will be bumped down the ranking of urgent issues).

It is a clever way of addressing concerns, and I have seen all of these used almost religiously over the years. Unfortunately, it typically has a high level of success, and the candidates are the ones who suffer. You wonder whether the clients just give up hope.

But you know, there will be people reading this who think that RPOs are the best thing since sliced data. They will be arguing that the idea of poor service is just the opinion of someone with an axe to grind. Ok, let me explain how it is that RPOs fall down, and how this all comes together to screw candidates.

Then make up your mind afterwards whether I have just plucked it all out of thin air.

So, buckle up your seatbelts and here we go.

§

Most recruiting operations use an ATS (an Applicant Tracking System) of one kind or another. A repository for candidate applications, which can show the status of 'live' advertised jobs. Some are designed more as databases rather than to support pipelines. These allow recruiters to see the number of applications per job, how many candidates have passed each stage, or how many have dropped out of the process.

Volume recruiters bank on their ATS because it would be impossible to keep on top of the volumes without it. It is not unusual for high-volume enterprises to almost wholly rely on such technology. Think of contact centres and their ACD/telephony reporting, together with Customer Relationship Management (CRM) platforms. This is essential technology.

In an ATS, high-level statuses are easily shown for at-a-glance reporting. You can see application totals for each role and numbers at each stage, and you can drill into each candidate record, where you can see application forms and copies of communications sent. Using these, you can tick-box candidates and perform bulk actions. It all makes sense, and you can see the potential for efficiencies.

Having said this, recruitment campaigns are not the same type of processes like pure contact centre communications activities, where statuses of lines are clear, and reporting is at the touch of a button. With pure contact centre work, you can see the one-dimensional lines of activity at any time:

x calls offered; y handled.

Average call length, x mins, and abandoned calls y%.

Agent A handled y calls with z call length.

Everything comes in on one dimension and it can be measured, analysed automatedly and presented.

Recruitment processes are much more complicated. Numerous processes and statuses can change at any moment in time, with people being taken out of a process or being put back in. Candidates can appeal decisions, or mistakes can be uncovered and rectified.

ATS systems work in such a way that before each stage, you have to pull a separate report on candidate statuses and then determine who is moved where in accordance with a management decision on pass marks. You then work from this report and ensure that the ATS statuses/actions match this.

It is a reconciliation task that represents one mighty crack, through which many a candidate has fallen.

And it is this separate process of pulling a report, filtering it, and reconciling it with your ATS that is full of holes. Black holes even, because you cannot begin to imagine how copious they are until some jumped-up middle-ranking bureaucrat is tearing you a new one while simultaneously spitting flames into it.

Lamentably, there is no safe mode in an ATS for bulk moving, so managers have to work from a separate list when preparing for bulk moves and then work through the 'live' ATS to process candidates. They cannot go into an ATS, put all the candidates onto their planned updated statuses and then, having checked that all candidates are on the right steps, press the big red button. It is a question of working through the list in real-time. If you come to the last action and you are expecting 25 candidates left and you have 10 to process, you will have made a mistake, and it will be a challenge to unpick.

Think of the shop assistant who counts your money into the till and then tells you that you are short. Too late to do a re-count.

Intelligent reporting can therefore be challenging because it can incorporate many variables. It might be straightforward to display at a high level how many people passed an online test, for example. But the salient question might be how many BME or disabled candidates passed. That might be crucial information for an assessment decision.

And that is not information that can be easily presented. It may also be confidential data that can be accessed only by those with certain permissions.

So, another level of reports – perhaps several – has to be constructed in order to complement the higher-level ATS displays so that managers can track the groups of candidates and display them correctly. Hold that thought for a moment.

Another key factor with reports is that they have to be built by those who are aligned with user thought processes in order to make the outputs intelligible.

Accordingly, you may need to express in a report that candidates have, let us say, passed an online test and are at the Interview stage. In the ATS you will have, beneath the top total: *Invited, Booked, Completed, Passed, Failed, Hold.* Or at least, if you do not have them, you will need to know them.

The report will need to see the series of steps closed down correctly or completed before it registers a number at the next step. This will prevent double counts. It may also calculate those at *Invited Interview* as the total of those who successfully completed the preceding stage. This in turn is determined by those stages being closed correctly.

In brief, reporting is determined by the fulfilment of criteria, not simply a straightforward observable reality.

Reports rely on whether candidates are processed correctly, and there will be many mini-steps in an ATS. While candidates may be at the right process step, this can screw reporting if the report fails to pull through candidates and if all those reported as *Pass* need to have fulfilled a selection of completed sub-steps.

It is a scary prospect to consider that as a candidate, you may miss out on your invitation – your only chance in an application process – because you are misprocessed and do not appear on a list. All because an ex-call centre bod with 30 minutes training, trained by a man, who was trained by a man – all of whom had only the same 30 minutes of ever-more-diluted training – drops a not inconsiderable bollock.

And by the time you chase up your update because you haven't heard anything, the process stage might be over.

If I had a £1 for every candidate lost in RPO oblivion by that method, I'd be, well, as wealthy as every RPO shareholder.

What then follows is the seemingly endless battle for reinstatement, which for reasons we all now know, can be challenging.

All the more so, given that tracking back communications can be difficult. An ATS will commonly use templated records, so as a candidate, you will have on your record the template (with fields populated) of the email you *should have received at the status you passed*, not a copy of the precise one you were actually sent.

Differences can arise if an advisor goes into your record and changes any text with a view to sending a communication manually. You could get a rejection (manually put together), but your record shows a pass. You then do not complete the next stage because you weren't invited. Your record says you were, but you did not complete the test.

You then receive a withdrawal notice for not completing a test by the deadline. You complain, but your candidate record is conclusive on the point and backs the RPO's version of events.

Here is some probably self-explanatory advice – keep all your communications, particularly as many organisations still use standalone Outlook, so a lot of the correspondence between you and them will be unconnected to your candidate record (you did not think that RPOs invested in fully integrated solutions, did you?) Even a conscientious manager looking into your complaint/query may not know how to track down all the pieces to substantiate your concerns.

Unfortunately for all the gloss, a lot of these RPOs run processes that are held together in the background by chewing gum. A lot of the time, online test results are completed on separate systems, with test results pulled onto an Excel sheet, and the results are flicked out to somebody to manually type into candidate records.

How many mistakes do you think get made there? More than just a few, I can tell you.

Reporting, which underpins so many decisions is a whole festering boil that urgently needs a lance and to be dressed in pertinent investment. Do not hold your breath though.

With an ATS, a report cannot just be built and then re-run ongoing. There is a certain amount of rebuilding every time and maintenance of data to ensure that candidates are on the right steps, with sub-steps completed in order. Without a doubt, given constraints on resources, this is not always done correctly.

Ad hoc reporting is limited and, apart from filterable data dumps, will almost certainly need to be ordered or be at least scheduled for self-service. The problem is that the variable nature of recruitment activity and queries arising from it make it impossible to predict exactly how data needs to be cut for purposes that may not yet have arisen, so there is generally an immediate limitation to standard reports.

Furthermore, ad hoc reporting can be risky because if it is done incorrectly, the reporting mechanism will needlessly explore the whole ATS database to search for data to pull, which can easily crash an ATS and freeze its everyday operations.

As if this were not enough, MI teams are usually woefully under-resourced, so reports arrive at the last moment before being due for review or for dispatch to clients. They will frequently have errors for all the above reasons, so will just get banged out regardless. This has several results.

Operational teams make big errors because they are using duff data...

Or the reports go out to stakeholders, who either make wrong decisions which come back into the operation...

Or *Account Managers* get set up for an Olympic-level shoeing on a subsequent conference call...

Or they will be delayed. In this case, managers have to explain campaign statuses without MI, which also qualifies them for a colossal beating...

And the reports – even if correct – are never really satisfactory. Clients either get MI that has too few columns so that they cannot understand what is happening, or they get too much detail, so they cannot see the wood for the trees. Either way, recruitment decisions off the back of the MI are often incorrect, and candidates lose out. For you the candidate, it means that nobody ever really knows what the heck is going on and your interests are neither protected by RPO nor the hiring manager.

The operations teams do sometimes step in to save the day though with their knowledge of the pipelines, allowing them to tweak error-laden reports.

Or do they?

Sometimes, particularly if candidates are being put back into the process, the high-level numbers can be tweaked. Sadly, as the diversity profiles of all those candidates will be unknown to the front-line troops, these will be skewed. As a result, while the amended reports look on one level to be ok, any decisions made on the basis of diversity categories will likely be on a false premise, for some candidates at least.

If you are one who has fallen through the cracks, it probably will not be discovered any time soon. And if it is, it will probably be at a stage when it will be more convenient that you stay forgotten.

Either because it is a major headache to discover a lost candidate when the vacancies have been filled or the issue involving you lands just at a point where the RPO is about to get tin-tacked if your case gets aired. It may be the case that a quick re-jigging of the data may allow the *Operations Manager* to jet-piss the final skid marks from the pan, i.e. your errant application.

§

So, let us consider how a report that needs to be reconciled can become immeasurably more complicated.

At the very start of a new campaign build, before the jobs are even advertised, administrators set up application forms using well-practised design shortcuts. If you have two or more identical jobs to advertise but in different locations, they might, for instance, just use one single ATS job, with a location dropdown on the form for the location preference.

You see, ATS administrators are as indolent as they are overworked. What is more, if they are offshore workers, they will be producing forms with half the questions missing and will neither have a clue nor will they care. A lot of RPOs offshore elements of set-up and support and do not even tell their clients! They are that dismissive of the hands that feed them. Not to mention non-cognizant of risks to data security. But I digress.

If they take this location shortcut, they cannot see clearly how many applicants they have had for each job. Some might decide to give a nominal 'score' to candidates for one location, say 100, which will then be clear in a column in the ATS, so you can pick them out as you scroll down.

However then, it will be a not inconsiderable drag having to re-sort columns to answer questions from clients on the phone who are tearing their hair out for updates.

The bigger ball-aches come though when pulling a report for a test stage. This is when you, the candidate, get unceremoniously dicked because all these shortcuts and bodged set-up steps come back to haunt and roger the RPO rigid.

Now please return to our held thoughts on reports and further candidate parameters that may need to be incorporated.

For example, think about a test stage for a *Disability Confident* scheme. They will have a list of candidates for location A, but on the list, they will have disabled candidates, those disabled with *RAs*, disabled who have selected the *Guaranteed Interview Scheme (GIS)*, disabled with *GIS* and *RAs*. These breakdowns will apply to all locations, so the complexity ratchets up considerably.

Who would've thunk it? Makes your rosebud pucker just thinking about the multifarious twists and turns that a process could take. And you with it.

All candidates have to be processed differently, and that is a lot of breakdowns that they have to reconcile with one high-level view on an ATS. It would be easier to draw a Birmingham motorway map.

And there are hundreds of these unfolding at any one time in any RPO, with a lot more complexity of variables.

And to think that my assertion that mistakes are common might be challenged by RPOs who claim that they oversee perfectly flowing processes with minimal errors?

I do not think I need to add anything else to the justification for my assertions — I will leave you to digest and to draw your own conclusions. But as a candidate within a volume process administered by an RPO? Be vigilant and very careful – I wish you all the luck in the world because very often that is what will mean the difference between fair and unfair.

So how do RPOs manage to twist and turn through fact and fiction and manipulate circumstances to their advantage? The answer lies in the way stakeholder relationships are structured and the concept of *Private and Public*.

15 – Venn Trick or Circles?

Private vs Public – a sociological insight into why shit happens.

Now is the time for a theoretical concept. My intention is not to bore you, but this is an important one even if, on reflection, it might have been dropped on you by Captain Obvious.

If you were fortunate enough to have studied Sociology (which means that at school you may have just not liked Science or Languages, so tilted your *Options* the other way), you may be familiar with the terminology of *public and private spheres*.

These terms are used by sociologists to describe two distinct realms in which members of society move freely on a day-to-day basis. The difference between them is as follows: *the public sphere* is thought of as a political domain where people come together to exchange ideas and information. A sphere that would be open to all. *The private sphere*, however, has boundaries and is enclosed, with limitations on those who are allowed to enter it. For example, this might be like a home.

You may have heard of a social scientist by the name of *Jürgen Habermas* who made the distinction between public and private spheres in 1962[x]. Public spheres are seen as the core of democracy, where members of the public can openly discuss and articulate ideas and concerns relating to societal needs. The great thing about the public sphere is that social status should be irrelevant and the important areas for consideration concern themselves with common interests, inclusivity and what is right and wrong. On the other side of the coin or, to be precise, the coin of society, is the private sphere where responsibilities centre on oneself and other close relations, for example, members of one's family. This should be free of the influence of governments and other social institutions.

Nevertheless, in spite of these theoretical delineations, what is private and what is public may change and flux over time and in different contexts. For example, up until recent years, some forms of domestic violence in the UK were seen as a de jure private concern. The law has now been changed so that criminal offences such as *coercive control* are now a public concern.

§

The world of recruitment reflects an interaction very much between candidates and recruiting organisations in both public and private spheres. Clearly, the matter of a job application is, by its very nature, private and confidential, so in effect, a bespoke private sphere is created, where, for example, individual applications or assessment performance are guaranteed absolute confidentiality. This process necessitates that candidates are truthful and act with integrity at all times, with this reciprocated by the hiring organisation. Indeed, some of the criteria for public sector recruitment, where there is the highest level of scrutiny on the actions of a prospective employer, will give absolute guarantees in relation to this.

However, the individual private spheres of candidates must fall within an overarching public sphere, where all candidates are aware of the role and the process. There are of course pockets of the private sphere that are unknown to either party within the private sphere, which is understandable and determined by decision-making at an individual level. Candidates may have information that they choose not to divulge and equally, recruiters may have information regarding, for example, their decision-making processes that they keep out of view. Nothing wrong with that at all.

Apologies for the dry analysis here, but it serves to categorise some ideas into some clear boxes that will help to explain what actually happens, once the game is afoot.

This is of course how everything should work in theory. Of course, recruiters may decide to cut their candidates out of the private sphere at particular points in the process for a multitude of reasons.

This could be by *ghosting* them (which incidentally is sometimes driven by candidates themselves who lose interest in a position) or perhaps by not divulging factual reasons for an application hitting the buffers. In these circumstances, candidates will undoubtedly feel a sense of dissatisfaction with the way the process has been handled, and indeed this kind of action on the part of recruiters has been a principal contributory factor in the downgrading of reputation for those working in the so-called recruitment industry.

As any candidate knows — irrespective of the safeguards, principles, and standards of the public sphere — a candidate can have the proverbial rug pulled out from underneath them in the private sphere, with limited options available for redress. Simply because of this: in order to make a successful claim against a recruiter, you need to be able to lay your hands on tangible evidence — a near-impossible task if the recruiter successfully battens down the hatches. And even with evidence, there are only certain courses of action for very specific reasons that are open to candidates. These primarily relate to discrimination on the basis of protected characteristics.

It is of course a sad and lamentable fact that rights and guarantees for citizens that are available for all can be circumvented by the ability to pick and choose how the process runs within this private domain. Unfortunately, that is the way of the world, and it is of course not unique to recruitment. Everything stands and falls on the question of evidence and its availability, which can be closely controlled by those who are up to no good. In particular, those who are sufficiently well-informed on process, the law and how to manipulate them. I make this point about public and private spheres primarily to assist analysis of how the sharp practices of recruitment are actually able to happen with almost unadulterated impunity.

But it is even more interesting when the context of an RPO relationship is factored into this model.

In this situation, the public sphere remains as is, as for any other recruitment situation. The added intricacy brought forth by the introduction of an RPO into the process is that the private sphere is effectively divided into two separate sections.

Firstly, you have the sub-sphere of the RPO and hiring manager or client relationship.

Then you have the sub-sphere of the RPO and candidate relationship.

Now as a candidate, you need to be aware that the RPO will do everything in its power to ensure that those two worlds do not meet. By ensuring that the candidate is unable to establish a relationship with the hiring manager organisation, the RPO can run the process however they like with very little chance of any comeback for them. That is not to say that RPOs set up recruitment processes with the specific intention of denying candidates opportunities.

However, it is undeniable that RPO processes are often managed by employees who are not qualified to do so, who are generally plucked from the wider contact centre population, and who have little sympathy or empathy for those candidates in the process. As a result of this, and indeed as a result of the combination of these factors, significant errors are made with alarming regularity.

When these come to light, the only point of contact that the candidate has is with the RPO itself. Now you do not need a degree in philosophy to work out how those complaints generally go. They are diverted, deflected, and minimised – however you would like to put it – in order to prevent the up-kicking of a stink, so to speak. RPOs are shitstorm navigators. It is what they do best.

There are many ways in which this can be done though one of the most effective means of negating a concern – and this is more appropriate where there is a tight recruitment timeline for the particular process – is to stall. Nothing is more convoluted or complex than simply elongating the time period between receipt of concern and answer – and then responding with a question of their own, perhaps for clarification, which in turn adds a further delay before resolution.

At a point in the future, by which time as far as the process is concerned it is a question of horses and stable doors, the RPO might even acknowledge that they had perhaps not handled the matter as well as they might (a rarity, but it happens). This will be the case if there is something fairly innocuous that the RPO can fess up to, and in doing so, demonstrate that they are not overly defensive and are willing to acknowledge errors. As an aside, I waxed lyrical over these shenanigans, in *Flypaper for Freaks*. This kind of subterfuge underpins much of my analysis on indeed anything.

§

So back to the plot, providing of course that we haven't yet lost it.

In any event, the candidate will realise at that point that even a victory in terms of the argument will be a Pyrrhic one. They would have missed the opportunity to obtain the role. In the event that this floats to the surface and the client becomes aware of the issue, the RPO will attempt to summarise in a sanitised version what has happened and rely heavily on the fact that contacts in the client organisation are so overworked (hence the reason why they may have decided to outsource in the first instance) that they accept the RPO summary, which in turn prevent hours of laborious legwork, for which they have little time or enthusiasm.

With a sturdy flush, it should all go down the pan, without having to wait for the cistern to refill.

Make no mistake, the connection between candidate and client or hiring organisation is the veritable bogeyman for the RPO organisation. They will do anything within their power to prevent that connection from being made. So as a candidate, you need to be very aware of when you are dealing with RPOs so that you can go route 1 directly to the hiring organisation in the event that the fun-and-games become apparent through any obvious heel-dragging when a problem arises.

Yes, it is a little awkward because everybody likes to be nice, particularly when they are engaging in a process and seeking a favourable outcome from it. Nonetheless, candidates need to remember that in dealing with an RPO, they are not dealing with a decision-maker who might reject them on a whim. The RPO is there, largely, to administer processes. They are not decision-makers, but they do rely heavily on automation and untrained staff who make mistakes that will largely go unnoticed. And when they are discovered, there is of course a clear incentive (namely the client relationship) why they will not want to acknowledge those errors to you readily. That is why you need to be on point to nip these problematic and thorny issues in the bud.

Now I do not want to be all doom and gloom, but where RPOs are involved in some form of decision-making, such as sifting CVs, the only hope you have in rectifying a poorly substantiated decision is if the client themselves are undertaking a process of review and moderation. Unfortunately, in such cases, these exercises would not involve the review of more than a 10% sample. After all, if you are using an RPO, why buy a dog if you are going to bark yourself?

And even more unfortunately, the review of CVs and application forms is already problematic owing to their subjective nature and dependence on the ability and understanding of the sifter. This will apply to those reviewers client-side as well as within the RPO though the level of incompetence will be proportionately higher with the latter.

Wherever you turn in recruitment, there is always somebody bigger and worse.

16 – Panel Beating

The joy of face-to-face interviews

So, the near impossible has happened. You have managed to squeeze yourself through the colon of the application process and you have dropped with a light *plop* into the interview pan.

Congratulations – it is an achievement in itself, take it from me.

So, what are interviews actually supposed to be?

Well, employers for all their faults do realise that it is best to meet someone first before offering them a contract of employment. Although that doesn't always happen! As the name implies, they are an opportunity for the prospective employer to look at the candidate and vice versa, based on relevant conversation and stimulated by questions that are designed to elicit information and give the other party an opportunity to enlighten the other on what they have to offer. Yes, that just about covers it.

The part *inter* means *within*, *between* or *among*. It is supposed to be a two-way process with benefits for either party.

Sounds reasonable? Indeed, it should. But alas, in the world of recruitment, nothing is quite as straightforward as it ought to be. There are some good reasons for this, some of which stem from good intentions. You see, there needs to be some structure which will more likely than not involve method and rigidity that determine exactly how things will run.

Interviews that are unstructured can lead to nothing more than chats over a cup of coffee, eliciting information from candidates that fails to get to the heart of their skills and capabilities and is scarcely comparable to that produced for other candidates. This can all frustrate attempts at establishing a fair process.

In order to address this, HR specialists have long since promoted structured interviews based on clear competencies that can be related directly to the job description of the role in question. I am sure that most people are familiar with the typical structure of a competency-based question, which will often begin with a *'tell me about a time when you...'*

A *competency* is a concept that links the three strands of *Knowledge, Skills, and Attitude*. You might have great interpersonal skills (skills) but will not be competent to join a company as a *Finance Manager* unless you also have adequate education/experience (knowledge) and the right temperament/behaviour (attitude). This is the science that supports the *competency-based interview (CBI)* methodology.

Structured *CBIs* are interviews where each question is designed to test competencies, and the candidate's answer is reviewed against set criteria and marked. If testing '*resilience*', the interviewers may ask the candidate to describe a time when they had to work under pressure and what they did. One of the ways in which candidates can structure a competency-based answer is by using the *STAR* method, where they outline the *situation*, *task*, *actions* and finally the *results*.

CBIs are however starting to be complemented - even usurped – by strengths-based questions and interviewing where interviewers will ask you what you enjoy doing and what invigorates you. How you deal with strengths-based questions will give a strong indication of what motivates you, what makes you perform well and the types of work to which you will be best suited.

For my part, this is a movement from the more structured to the less structured interview question format, where interviewers understand more about organisational fit than anything else.

Competency-based questions look on the face of it to be the most appropriate questions to put to a candidate because the alternative might well be *conditional questions* which are really then just drawing on a candidate's imagination about what they think they *might* do in comparison with the clarity of what we know *they have done*.

However, competency questions in practice are fraught with difficulties themselves. Firstly, candidates simply invent examples of fantastic things that they have done and then trot them out parrot-fashion when the familiar questions are put to them at the interview.

In this sense, they are of little greater value than the hypothetical *conditional questions*. I have witnessed brilliant interview performances from candidates citing examples of their previous careers, whereas I know for a fact that the majority of what they have said is pure fiction. Sometimes I had specific knowledge that what happened did not involve them and at other times it just did not add up.

But let us assume for a moment that a competency-based format is not susceptible to that kind of manipulation. Just for a moment.

§

In a typical assessment process, or at least one that has been correctly run, the candidates will be aware of the competencies that are relevant to the role, having read them in the *job description* or *person specification*.

Accordingly, these are likely to form the backbone of anything that a candidate will have to face during an interview. And when asking questions during the interview, the panel should state clearly which competency they are hoping to test, prior to posing the relevant question. If they decide not to, then the candidate may have some difficulty in ascertaining precisely which competency is being tested by the question and therefore may not produce either an appropriate example or an answer that is structured in a way that fully addresses the competency implied in the question.

At that point, the panel may start to experience moments of awkward silence or receive answers that fall below expected standards or do not reflect the true capability of the candidate. In such circumstances, we are starting to enter the realms of unreliability in relation to interview questions. So, while the questions themselves may be reliable, it is the framing of the questions that leads to unreliability. Unfortunately for the candidate, any third party reviewing the answers, for example, in a wash-up session following the assessments, will simply see an answer that may not fulfil the requirements of the question. *Et voilà*, here is one of the problems with this type of situation. The documentation reflects something very different from the wider context of reality.

And this is how candidates lose out.

Furthermore, and *encore* unfortunate for the candidates, interviewers do like to dress up questions slightly differently and re-phrase them in order to hide the competencies that they are actually seeking to test. Now I can kind of see the logic of that because while conducting a structured interview, with the intention that all candidates are asked the same questions (so they will therefore be able to collect data that will stand up to comparability), the panel will not want everything to seem stilted and unnatural.

Unfortunately, in changing the wording of a carefully constructed question, the meaning of questions has an unfortunate habit of morphing in its entirety, with candidates then taking a very different approach in the formulation of their answers. This may mean that candidates are deemed to have answered inappropriately, whereas in fact they have perfectly analysed the question that was actually. With carefully scripted and structured questions, those questions are tested for validity and reliability. This means that the questions will test what they purport to test and that they will be solid enough to be interpreted in the same way by all candidates. Once again, when panel members go rogue, the questions become unreliable as do the records of those questions.

And it is only the candidates who lose out.

§

Alternatively, you can get panels who are so robotic in their approach that they divvy up the questions and then go up and down the line simply reading the questions out like it is the first time they have ever seen them. And of course, in many cases, it *will be* the first time they have ever seen them. The problem here is that the interview process becomes so mechanical that candidates feel as if they are sitting in an empty room. Or that while they are being asked questions, they are not really sure who they are talking to because the questions seem like they have come from somewhere else and the answers that candidates are giving are just blowing into the ether. And if the panel members are not truly engaged in the questions, how can they fully appreciate the extent of the answers that the candidates give?

As a result, the notes they take down may not necessarily capture the salient points that the candidates are making. I can recall one incident myself when the panel members mechanically read out the pre-prepared questions and the lead interviewer, bearded Tom, typed notes, glassy-eyed as if he were a visually impaired court stenographer. Throughout the whole ninety-minute interaction, the only thing really going through my head was if any of my words were actually sinking in.

I was also at the time trying to get to grips with the fact that they had given me a chair with wheels on it which, when you are shuffling slightly uncomfortably in your seat owing to the disengaged and non-responsive body language of the panel, made it a miracle that I did not manoeuvre myself subconsciously out of the door.

Needless to say, I was not successful in achieving an invitation to draw a future stipend from that clan of clowns.

But before you offer your condolences and your sympathies, I have already begun the preparation for the groundwork of this book. Therefore, the headspace I was occupying was absolutely conducive to a positive mental attitude. To reverse that popular maxim, when you are in a room and you can see all the crazy people, there is an increasing possibility that you are not the crazy one yourself. Or at least, that is the straw of respectability at which I was determined to grasp. And I am still smiling.

All these examples demonstrate how the process of running an interview may well lead to some serious disconnects and inconsistencies.

The most striking of these is the gap between what candidates are asked and what is recorded as having been asked, which may be tangibly different. I can remember in one atrociously managed interview when I was asked a question about *'management styles'*, which I answered in a particular way and then later in the same interview the other interviewer referred back to my answer on *'leadership styles'*. Now those are two very different questions, so it is possible that in the interview record there were notes about my thoughts on *situational management* under a question on *leadership style*.

But that is not reflective of what was asked, and the discrepancy meant that I would not likely score very highly. I never did find out because I did not get any feedback – more on that later. Clearly though, any third-party moderating would have looked at the official question and assumed that, as a candidate, I had not understood it. In fact, it was the case that the question was incorrectly asked. I wish I'd picked them up on it, but at that stage in the interview, which had been a tough one up to that point, I was hanging on for dear life in an attempt to establish a high level of credibility. And to be honest, when the chips are down, your starting point is actually to doubt yourself and not the panel.

You see, the panel will hold a position of absolute authority in any process. What is more, whatever they choose to record or not record will define your strength as a candidate. Not your knowledge, not your opinions, not the viewpoints of those who know you best. *What they record*.

This is of course inextricably linked with *what they understand*. I recall a delightful example of a panel where the spellbindingly dim HR makeweight, Nikki (not Nicola, of course), became flummoxed by the references to my *contribution* when one of the other panel members posed a question about the commercial success of my department. She then asked incredulously whether I would seriously consider making up any profit gaps by returning parts of my own salary to the bottom line.

Fortunately, another panel member stepped in with a helpful, albeit dry, definition of *contribution* as *the amount of earnings remaining after all direct costs have been subtracted from revenue.*

The bland leading the blond, so to speak. Nikki did not offer anything further during that particular exercise.

But back to the main points in question, the capability of the panel and the implications thereof.

If you are faced with a mundane question regarding any competency and choose to attack that with a theory that is more involved than the usual drivel trotted out by the vast majority, you need to be sure that the panel are at the same level in terms of intellect.

If they are not and cannot grasp the points you are making, you will run the risk of being marked down on *communication skills. For not making yourself clear.* I have also been part of panels in these situations when members have pointed out that (stellar) candidates have not only performed poorly on clarity but have omitted to demonstrate 'the essentials', i.e. the mediocre twaddle that the fat part of the bell curve churns forth.

So dire panels will penalise great candidates because they cannot recognise brilliance and think that parrot-fashioned mediocrity is *'what good looks like'.*

It's hardly pushing the boundaries on hiring great talent, is it?

§

So now we arrive at the emergence of *strengths questions*. These have been brought in to address the question of potential while recognising that not all candidates, particularly those who have been disadvantaged, will have had the opportunity to demonstrate competency-related achievements.

Sounds like a positive move to boost *social mobility* and *D&I*.

Oh dear. It is also quite worryingly a way of disguising the fact that *motivational fit* is becoming one of the most-emphasised qualities that panels take on board, prior to making a selection decision. I guess people also recognise that an interview process too reliant on competency questions can be mastered and exploited by those who are disingenuous.

The problem with *strengths questions* is that nobody really knows how to position them to candidates, or indeed how to grade them effectively with any degree of consistency. Some of the public sector organisations who are now using *strengths questions* in tandem with, ahem, *behavioural questions* end up with wash-up sessions where frankly they might as well be spinning a bottle to select which candidate to appoint. In many cases they end up appointing the candidate who is, in the opinion of the hiring manager, *the best fit*.

And *behavioural questions*? Yep, these are *competency questions*, dressed up in a different guise. And woe betide anyone who regresses and uses the C-word. And I do not mean *clown* unless of course you are referring to the panel members themselves.

Now this whole question of motivational fit really does reflect a misplaced sense of self-importance on the part of organisations, who expect candidates to know the ins and outs of who they are and what they do, to the extent that it is now a common prerequisite for selection. The number of times I have witnessed candidates being downgraded because they did not know considerable amounts of information or sufficiently accurate information about a company's business, well, even I cannot believe it myself sometimes. It is buffoonery at its most majestic.

Even the most passionate, engaged and personally motivated individuals will not get far until they have ticked all the boxes of what the ever-increasingly prevalent sub-psychotic middle- and senior managers deem to be a motivational fit that is devotedly personal to their brand and exudes almost encyclopaedic sycophancy.

It is tragic. But the key to the door of the cloistered clown coteries of low-rent and reality-disconnected organisations.

All this stems from the paranoia of senior management teams who cannot believe that the world exists outside the four walls of their organisations. As a result, their baseline expectation is that anybody who is interested in joining their organisation is doing so because candidates are completely wedded to the same ideology that drives them as senior managers.

They just do not get it.

§

Candidates are keen to earn a living, so anything where they can work and earn an acceptable level of salary, which is convenient to them in terms of location and whose business is not too much of an affront to any particularly strongly held views that they might have, then the chances are they will apply.

Who gives a shit whether they know who your key clients are or how much profit you made last year? They can pick up all that stuff once they are in post and raring to go. But more often than not, people who do not score so highly in their motivational fit questions will not progress one step further forward. But it bears out what I have previously said.

A lot of these organisations would rather fail in the company of acolytes who hang on their every word than bring in people who are exceptional at their jobs (but do not treat the senior management teams like they were idols to be worshipped).

The question of motivational fit has however taken a more sinister turn in the inappropriate use of *personality tests* for candidates. Again, I have been given personality tests, the results for which had been produced at the start of an interview, which left me in no doubt that before even answering a single question, I was already off on the wrong foot. And that is after being sent the questionnaire and being told that it would have no impact on any decision-making. Not only is that inherently stupid in itself because it plays right into the *halo and horns* mode of operation, but it is also highly disingenuous.

Moreover, the person who runs through your answers and who interprets the findings of the questionnaire is typically not an occupational psychologist, but some middle-ranking HR grunt (with *Director title* to boot), who possibly went on a half-day course on personality testing, run by one of these HR pop-up consultancy firms, offering their 'accreditations' in *NLP* and other pseudo-scientific claptrap.

Unfortunately, having paid their £599 plus VAT, these thought-mongfish are sitting in front of you, having assumed all of the character traits, demeanour, and authority of a consultant psychiatrist, while they try to convince you like some kind of low-rent cold reader that they understand you better than you understand yourself.

For the interviewer though, it allows them to use all the power they possess within the structures they define to objectify you and categorise you in a manner that suits their perspective. It is precisely what *Michel Foucault* describes when he talks about the roles of schools, prisons, hospitals, and other institutions[xi]. An assertion, not without criticism, that institutions and processes associated with them exist to control and categorise rather than to achieve their stated aims.

And of course, for the interviewers, such categorisations, particularly if they can get you to agree with them during the interview itself, provide a wonderful justification for decisions taken and a perfectly apt cleansing of any sense of guilt on the very remote off chance that they may pause at some stage for a moment of self-reflection and consideration of their own bias.

What happens in the delivery of interviews might be seen as a *personalised enactment* of an established role. This is where individuals are given the responsibility to own a mundane task and decide to perform it in such a way as to fulfil a performed action in practice, driven by a set of internalised beliefs or perspectives.

In summary, you will see people who seek to control others in situations where they are given the power to do so. It is these attitudes that provide personal motivation to act in the ways that they do, which on a wider scale can shape normalised behaviours in organisations and even industries. I am sure you can think of many examples, where people do their job strictly speaking to the letter, but their manner of delivery betrays the desire to dominate and to make the situation as unpleasant as possible.

As a result of them doing it to the letter, they have a certain amount of official justification for their actions, for which they can neither be criticised nor challenged.

Computer says no.

You see in many respects, some people are given the task of hosting or participating in an interview and they deliver that task. In doing so, and in failing to interact with the individuals in front of them in a sympathetic manner, the quality of the conversation means that such interviews fundamentally fail to meet their stated objectives and opportunities are missed for both organisations and candidates. But in a world where documentation reigns supreme, those interviews will be professionally recorded and will not even remotely be challenged within the context of actually what they were intended to achieve. It is a crazy, crazy, world and these individual powerplays feature in interviews every day and can be the difference between success and failure for all concerned.

§

But for me personally, nothing could ever beat the moment at the end of one interview when the hiring manager produced a well-worn packet of cards (which looked like a gift from a Christmas Cracker) and proceeded to lay them out in front of me with the words, *'this is something I like to do with all candidates at the end of interviews'*. Well, what was going to follow could have been anything of a reputable or disreputable nature, but it was in fact four coloured cards (red, green, blue, and yellow), each representing a series of personality-related traits, which I was invited to rank in terms of relevance to my own personality. We were in *De Bono Hat* territory, administered by some cockwomble bottom-feeder, who was seeing out his final years before trousering his public sector pension.

At this point, I knew the gaffe was blown and that this kind of pseudoscientific twaddle was going to be the final hook on which to hang the reasons for my rejection. It was evident that at the end of the day, they could draw a conclusion based on whichever way the wind needed to blow. And yes, the guy who would no doubt be making the decision had no formal psychological qualifications whatsoever.

What a time to be alive.

There was a moment of levity in my mind at least when he followed up that question and asked me, '*what colours I would expect to see when I went out into the wider office'.* I immediately thought that I would probably see some black people and possibly some Chinese. But I did manage to stick to the script and put together an answer relating to his paper-hat Crackerjack bullshit.

As a candidate, you should never be surprised at the kind of weird and inane turd that recruiters pull out of the doggy bag. Everybody is an expert on everything. Since the era of *New Labour*, there have never been shortages of the *Everyman* in every walk of life. Trying to be everything, for everybody. It is probably the only way they can feel as if they are surviving. What actually they need to do is be themselves and work hard at something.

§

Understandably, these are the ways in which the structures of interviews are subverted in practice by inconsistencies taken by interviewers. But when you think back to the raison d'être of interviews that we looked at at the beginning of this chapter, you would think that interviewers would be keen to put people at ease so that they were sufficiently relaxed and comfortable to give it their best shot and communicate as effectively as possible.

After all, that would be a prerequisite for facilitating any two-way interaction for the benefit of all parties. But time after time, you will enter a room where your interview takes place, to be met by a stony-faced panel of individuals who do everything they can to reinforce the imbalance of power in that room.

At the end of the day, they are fluffily secure in their roles within the organisation, and you are the one who is pitching or making the case for employment. It never ceases to amaze me how interviewers will switch off all normal and socially agreeable body language and gestures as if they do not feel it is appropriate to be a member of the human race during a face-to-face stage in the process. They almost seem to forget that through their demeanour, they too are selling the organisation to the candidates, who will frequently feel that this is a company that they will not want to join even if presented with an offer at the end of it.

Of course, the reality for candidates is that interviewers are often plucked from the business at relatively short notice, to interview you when in fact they have more pressing and important business to attend to in their everyday jobs. It probably helps to explain why interviews are blandly read off scripts and how batches of questions are divvied up and why the progress of the interview shifts down the line of panel members and back again, like the dishes at *Yo Sushi!* that everybody has a look at, but nobody really wants to select. On occasions, as I may already have noted, the attendees at such interview panels do not have the slightest clue about what it takes to perform in the role for which you are applying. They tend to ask absolutely inane questions relating to their own area of expertise, into contact with which you will come once in a blue moon and situations where you would require absolutely no specialist knowledge.

Those people, in their notes, will often write very middle-of-the-road accounts of what you have said in your interview, so they can jump either way depending on the particular bent of the *Panel Chair* or decision-maker. What is certain is that they will not be doing you any favours in terms of sticking their necks out to recommend you for a position. In some cases, they will be savvy enough to have read the albeit implicit guidance from the more senior members of the panel and will have worked out in advance whether you are a favoured candidate or not and will comment accordingly.

Sometimes the panels will comprise a mix that includes potential peers or even potential subordinates in the hiring organisation. It is beyond mental. Again, it is all linked in with potential fit rather than measuring your ability and it opens the door for people to block your appointment if they see you as a potential threat to their comfy, cloistered existence.

Again, these hiring organisations just get swept away by their own funky hug-tastic notions of inclusive decision-making that they lose sight of the glaring gaps in the essential rationale. Hire the best person for the job.

§

The one undisputed joy of interviews is truly that, aside from having to field a barrage of one-directional questions, you do get the opportunity to ask your questions at the end. Of course, the questioning is hardly balanced. You have to face batshit question after batshit question for 95% of the interview and then have 5 minutes at the end *if there is anything, YOU'D like to ask US.*

It is hardly an equal opportunity for candidates to probe panels on *their* credentials.

How I would love to see a candidate take the opportunity to pull out a list of 8 to 10 competency questions of their own to put to the interview panel.

'So, Tom, would you please tell me about a time when you interviewed an excellent candidate who was actually more qualified and talented than you? How did you cope with that?

> *'Well, I just looked straight through him and continued to type up some inane bullshit to satisfy the moderation team'.*

I wonder how many members of such a panel would actually progress to answer such questions, were they presented? None. Maybe I'll apply for a horseshit role and give it a whirl. Providing I get through the sift, that is!

They would not play ball though because the norm for questions from the candidate at this stage is simply to ask for additional insight in relation to the organisation or the direction of the organisation in order to demonstrate some of the research they may have done. Or as you might have guessed, to build on the matter of motivational fit. It is certainly not to question the competence of the interview panel, but for many of us who have turned down positions in the past, the competence of the organisation is something that we will already have inferred from the quality of questions asked to us in the first instance.

Far from being opportunities for candidates to get to know organisations, or even for panels to dig deep into candidates, interviews are simply another structure put in place so that organisations can demonstrate that a fair and equitable process has taken place.

Panels are put together to show that decisions are made by bringing together diverse perspectives and achieving consensus, and data is collected under specified categories for all candidates so that the record of performance can be compared between candidates and against set criteria.

In practice, interviews are flawed at almost every turn. The decision on whether to employ you will be taken, at the very latest, during the first 60 seconds of your interview, possibly even before the fabric of your trousers has touched upon the seat of your inappropriately wheeled chair. And if they have sent you a personality questionnaire beforehand, with assurances that it is for background information only, you can be sure that the decision will have been reached before you have even purchased your train tickets.

§

A lot of recruitment experts will differentiate between the types of interview in relation to the format that is chosen. *Panel interviews*, which can be defined as having two or more interviewers in the room, are favoured by organisations that wish to eliminate personal bias from the assessment process. It is also hoped that two heads are better than one and that different interviewers will pick up on the full range of strengths or weaknesses and anything else so that a fairer result can be achieved. They are also thought of as being useful when a strong level of expertise in conducting interviews is not as readily available within the organisation.

Of course, there is also an advantage in that, while one interviewer is talking, the other can write up their notes more comprehensively. But I am not sure that this outweighs the disadvantages for the candidate, as I have already outlined. Some of these interviewers are simply reading scripts and are complacent, to say the least.

It also becomes quite overwhelming for candidates, already in unfamiliar surroundings, to be faced with a row of expressionless faces and little to offer in terms of interpersonal warmth. Not always the case with panels but certainly more familiar than unusual.

Individual interviews are of course risky in relation to bias. The way the interview is conducted, the scarcity of notes or at least pertinent facts and the risk that they may not be accurately recorded all feature as strong reasons why organisations tend to avoid them.

In fact, I am pretty sure that most recruitment organisations conducting interviews at the latter stage of the process will completely disavow them. That is not however to say that initial screening interviews would not take place on a one-to-one basis. Indeed, that is the norm for some processes.

I myself was interviewed once in a most bizarre situation when I had been invited to attend what the employer, or should I say prospective employer, had termed to be a focus group with incumbent employees. When I entered the room there was, after initial introductions, an instruction to turn over a piece of paper on which was printed a brief business problem. I was then asked for my thoughts on how I would address that (hitherto unseen) problem and subjected to 45 minutes of quick-fire questions on the subject at hand. A room full of jobsworth bureaucrats who all seemed to be shitting it more than I was.

I am not sure what I would call that type of interview, but it certainly was not a focus group. I didn't particularly struggle because fortuitously I was very familiar with the problem at hand. Though, for some candidates, I am sure that that would have been a crash-and-burn moment. What is more, nobody in the group took notes, so you have to wonder how any of the candidates were assessed on that occasion.

It was certainly bizarre and an example of how organisations can sometimes go rogue in running so-called assessments that are likely to be wholly devoid of structure, objectivity, and comparability.

The great irony of interviewing is, like all these recruitment processes, that intuitively they make sense. Organisations shore up that rationale with processes, which again (largely) stand up at the design stage. It all unravels though in the practical application.

However, the problem for candidates is that few notice, and even fewer care.

17 – Hanging on the Telephone

Telephone Interviews – an early opportunity for discovery

Interviewing is, of course, not always conducted in person.

Well, thank The Lord for that. At least you will be spared from some of the unimaginable angst that a mere presence in the same room as some of these clowns will bring.

As a candidate, you will doubtless by now be familiar with the use of *telephone interviews (TIVs)* during the earlier stages of an assessment process. These are valued by recruiters because they help filter out the weaker candidates on the basis of something more substantial than a simple capability test. It also enables the recruiter to see the candidate brought to life in a way that a CV or application form can never deliver.

Interviews over the telephone provide an insight into character and personality that would otherwise not be provided at these early stages. Of course, these are less expensive than face-to-face interviews, are quicker and altogether involve less effort for both you and the candidate. As a candidate, particularly if you are a certain geographical distance away, you get the opportunity to start to make your case for employment without incurring unnecessary costs.

Everyone's a winner, baby.

But for you as a candidate, there may be some challenges that you need to overcome. Firstly, they are not as convenient as you might be led to believe because you need to make sure that you have time allotted for the interview that is uninterrupted, and you also need to guarantee (assuming mobile phones are involved) a quality signal for the telephone conversation itself. It is also difficult to achieve rapport during a TIV (although most will formally grade you are the extent to which you achieve this), which is arguably more easily done face-to-face.

You may also not have a tremendous amount of choice of interview slots because you will have to schedule your interview outside of your existing working hours. But, when all is said and done, these TIVs, as they are indeed ubiquitously known, bring forth an opportunity to shine just a little brighter than via your two-page CV which will be skim-read for thirty seconds max.

As a candidate I have some suggestions for you, should you be called upon to undertake a TIV. Firstly, keep to the point. Listen to the questions and answer them concisely. You need to understand that during any given day, there will be an ongoing chain of appointments that your interviewer will need to keep. Some of these contact centres will give their interviewers 15 back-to-back interviews per day.

Yes, we are back in the domain of quantity over quality, but that is how they roll in shitebox call centre land. They have a gun to their head to keep to times and, in spite of their best intentions to self-motivate, there is a high chance that they will be feeling personally at a low ebb by the time they join the call.

Notwithstanding all of this, they will be performing miracles, so will be on time for you and almost certainly sounding chipper. They do their best to approach matters in a professional manner and should aim to help you put your best foot forward.

So, it is vital that they capture relative and relevant information and that they have as much time as possible to present the appropriate questions to you. You just need to be aware that anything irrelevant that you say will not score you any marks. While it is certainly the case that you have earned your right to a TIV by progressing to this stage in the process, you would not be making the best use of that time in blurting out irrelevant information.

You may certainly encounter interviewers who are quite to the point in bringing you back on track, to the extent that you will be interrupted and stopped if you are drifting too far from the subject at hand. Do not under any circumstances get antagonised by this. It is not an example of rudeness but undoubtedly in your best interest. I am aware of a number of TIVs that have gone downhill quite quickly because candidates acted adversely to this.

Also, do not attempt to multitask during a TIV, by carrying on with some other activity that you had planned such as searching the Internet or writing an email. Be absolutely in no doubt that anything other than your undivided attention will impact your performance during the interview.

Your brain cannot split off so that you can effectively read one thing and say another with conviction. That is a fact, and if you try to convince yourself that it can, you are heading for a fall. It only works on conference calls when you are not required to constantly speak. And we've all experienced that crushing moment when you hear your name spoken with raised intonation. That moment when a question has been posed to you, and you have not the slightest *Scooby* what preceded it.

You cannot be that person on a TIV, with your trousers down around your ankles. Even if you are not unmasked as completely, your divided attention is likely to be apparent to the interviewer who may well and quite rightly decide that your level of interest in the role is not what you purport it to be.

One additional dimension that may come into play might be the offer of a real-time interview via video conference, like Skype.

I would view these very much as a face-to-face session though there will be a lack of micro-expressions that you can often interpret to your advantage when close-up in the same room. You also need to consider what is behind you in the room, particularly as the panel may zoom in on visible detail in your house. You may be something of an amateur historian, but they may have concerns about your copy of *Mein Kampf* on the bookshelf behind you. Also, make sure you acclimatise to any interaction delays caused by network connections. If you talk over your panel in haste, it may increase their frustration and create an unwarranted and unwanted impression.

§

You should also use the TIV to check any salient facts and to gather any information that you may have missed during earlier stages in the process. It may be that you are simply directed back to candidate application packs that are available online or something similar, and you can of course acknowledge that you may have momentarily forgotten where that information was if you feel a little awkward at being reminded that you should have already seen it. You may encounter interviewers who get somewhat pissy and self-righteous but try not to get drawn into any confrontations because, at the end of the day, they are the ones who will be assigning grades to your performance.

And these are grades that will likely not be moderated by anyone else.

You may well become familiar with some of the stock phrases and scripted responses that *telephone interviewers* sometimes throw back at you. The rather stilted and robotic interactions in everyday life are simply natural and spontaneous.

For example, invariably your *telephone interviewer* will ask, *'how you are today?'*, at which point you would I am sure respond, *'very well thank you, and yourself?'*. You will then almost certainly be going to hear something along the lines of, *'I am very well; thank you thank you for asking'*.

Make no mistake, that is likely to sound exceedingly unnatural and plastic. But try not to let that seep into your demeanour because it will simply be something that all advisers are instructed to say and for which they will likely be assessed themselves if the interview is being recorded. It is not them but some self-important contact centre manager with the intellect of a grape who has read about the importance of scripting in an article they found on *Bing* and has not realised that such scripts do not go down well in the real world. Hey ho.

Contact centres of the world are full of people who think that these interactions work. Like the retail managers who think that customers appreciate being welcomed into stores by their sub-moron staff who then cannot cope with the most basic question you ask off-script. It is just another chapter in the obsession with the concept that *standardisation equals service*. You would have thought that the retail outlets going bust would have taught them, but as we have discussed here, they go into denial and even escalate their commitment to failed people and processes.

§

The only other things I would add about *TIVs* are these: firstly, your punctuality. Be available when the interviewer calls because you do not want to be senselessly shooting yourself in the foot by displaying anything that could be interpreted as unprofessionalism or lack of interest, which will see your grade go south.

Secondly, be aware that such interviews are almost certainly going to be recorded even though unlikely to be listened to, unless as part of an advisor's few monitored interviews per month, or even less likely as part of a moderated sample. This creates an opportunity for you to leverage some recourse, should things go awry on the part of the interviewer.

Once again, if you are going to raise concerns, first of all ascertain whether or not it is an agency or an RPO that is conducting the TIV on behalf of a client, i.e. the organisation owning the role for which you are applying. Then, make sure you make your complaint rockets directly to the hiring organisation. This should ensure that the RPO or agency is on the back foot and is under pressure of time to pull that recording and provide it. If you go to the agency first, they may provide a holding response for you while they investigate the matter. This gives them the opportunity to pull the recording, listen to it, and if shocking, come up with a feasible reason why the recording cannot be retrieved. You will then find yourselves high and dry in relation to any further escalation or resolution of the issue at hand.

The most common reasons for the inability to pull a recorded *TIV* will be an intermittent fault or the inability to identify your call in the system. By the time you have debated the ins and outs of this, the process will have moved on and the intensity of your interest in pursuing the matter will likely have diluted. It never helps when you are arguing a case, and you know that the likelihood of encouraging and covering corroborating evidence has been substantially minimised. Particularly when you know that the ship has sailed and that your reinstatement is likely to be no longer practical. Always make sure you are on the front foot.

One final word on TIVs. Always structure your answers based on *STAR* or a similar model, emphasising what you did, not what the group or wider team achieved and be clear on quantitative results. That way, the interviewer has a straightforward job in getting into the notes your own clear contributions that are connected to some tangible benefits.

That is what the hiring organisation will be looking for.

18 – Video Killed the Audio Star

The tentative emergence of Video Interviews

It was inevitable that, having explored TIVs as an option, the pressures of cost and convenience would press through a fresher alternative onto the agendas of recruiters.

So, having looked at the popular features of TIVs, we now come to the emerging inclusion of *video interviews* (or *VIVs*) into recruitment processes. Let me first tell you why VIVs came to the fore and why they are so popular. There are two reasons.

The first relates to cost. A VIV will be structured in such a way that after clicking on the invitation link, the questions appear on the screen in front of the candidate, who then proceeds to answer them. Accordingly, you do not have the interactions on either side that you would have in a TIV. Therefore, when assessing the responses after the fact, there is less for the recruitment advisor to review and of course, nothing for them to do in relation to actually receiving your completed responses. You simply record your responses, press <submit>, and that is it.

The cost of setting up a VIV link is minimal, and licenses can be obtained from a range of suppliers with very low associated unit costs for hosting the interviews on their system. These third-party costs, combined with less time required to assess the interviews, allow the VIV to stack up very favourably in comparison with a TIV.

The other bonus for the recruiter is that the resources required to assess and conduct this stage of the process can be flattened out during any working day. That is to say, the challenges of *availability* in terms of time and resources of interviewer and interviewee are largely eliminated. It is simply a question of identifying a window during which the VIVs need to be completed and sending the links to the interviewees. The recruiters are then free to allocate a period of time after that window in which to review and score the submissions.

So VIVs are absolutely a favourite for recruiters. They are great for reducing candidate numbers with all of the benefits of processing high volumes of candidates during a short period of time. And they suck up fewer resources and bring fewer administrative challenges than TIVs with their associated scheduling.

Of course, another bonus is that the assessor can actually see the candidate, so you can get a more rounded picture of them and should be able to tell whether or not they are being assisted by notes, which would not necessarily be detectable on a TIV.

§

One other happy beta effect of this channel is that VIV*s* do return a higher percentage of self-deselection. Approximately one-third of candidates do not proceed to take the test. There is no strong body of evidence to clarify why, but it is likely that the pressure of being recorded on camera and having to get structured answers out within a very short window of time proves to be just too daunting for some. Not to mention feeling a little weird at having to sustain motivated and bubbly answers for 20-odd minutes while looking at a screen.

Of course, recruiters will yammer on about the *You Tube* generation and Millennials loving to create content as their justification for using VIV*s*, but it is all poppycock. The number one consideration is cost.

The other huge benefit is that by using the VIV, they can reduce numbers sharply without the accentuated threat of adverse impact, which kills two birds with a single stone.

People certainly do report that it is particularly uncomfortable self-filming and, contrary to the idea that every assessment process should be designed to get the best out of candidates, the VIV may well fail at the first hurdle. Moreover, the personal bias of assessors may well work against you, and we are not even talking about discrimination based on protected characteristics. The assessor may just not like the look of you and at this stage in the process, where there are high volumes of candidates, you need to understand that there may well again be very little moderation or checking of assessor performance at this stage.

Notwithstanding the possible issues with prejudice, there are also the now well-established challenges in relation to assessor capability. As a candidate, your application may be at risk as a result of any or a combination of these factors.

Unlike TIVs though, a slippery agency or RPO can hardly deny that your interview was recorded successfully. You will therefore have a lot more opportunity for redress if the results you receive are overwhelmingly at odds with your own perception of your performance.

§

You should also be aware that most recruiters will have an alternative *TIV* script to use (with exactly the same questions) if you are shuddering too uncontrollably at the prospect of a VIV, or if you do not have the technical equipment readily available to record one. You will be amazed that I have heard of recruiters asking candidates to use the facilities at public libraries for VIV*s*.

Who says that recruiter empathy is a thing of the past?

Never underestimate the ability of a recruiter to wholly lose their grip on reality. If you receive the sort of advice that could have come from somebody on high levels of prescription medication, escalate to the HR team in the hiring organisation or even the CEO. That usually gets the juices flowing (yours and theirs).

One area with VIV*s* where candidates can fall down is not keeping to the point. Unlike TIVs, however, you do not have an interviewer present who is prompting you to keep you on track or to encourage you to provide more information if your responses are deemed to be somewhat light in terms of content. That is why as a video interviewee, you need to be absolutely focused and use the one or two minutes to read the question when it is presented, to structure your response in your mind and be clear and concise in your delivery. Speak in plain English or run the risk that the person assessing you will mark you down because they will not have the opportunity for clarification.

§

What is certain though is that VIVs tend to polarise candidate opinion. They either love them, or they hate them. As a final note of caution, I would encourage those who have disabilities that may make participating in a VIV problematic, to contact the recruiter at the earliest opportunity. As I have already mentioned, it is now established common practice that a TIV would be offered as an alternative and you will have to deal with few, if any, hurdles in order to get agreement on this.

So, with VIVs, remember this. If you love that sort of thing, fill your boots, but be disciplined with the conciseness of your responses.

VIVs are great for a corroborated complaint if you have one because those rogue RPOs cannot hide the evidence so easily.

And if you do not fancy it, speak up loudly and you can get the TIV that will suit you, and your chances, much better.

One final word though. If you decide to record your VIV early in the morning and you put on only your shirt and tie, remember to press <submit>, and close down the program before getting up to make yourself a cup of tea.

It is not unheard of for partially dressed interviewees to reveal more than just their competency strengths after they believe the camera has stopped rolling.

19 – Centres of Gravitas

'In the red corner, weighing in with relentless popularity, the undisputed champion of the recruitment and selection world – Assessment Centres'

You could not write anything about candidate experience without noting the omniscience of *assessment centres* (ACs) in processes the length and breadth of the country. Nobody questions their inclusion in recruitment processes because they are so routinely relied upon. Part of the recruitment furniture, no less.

Indeed, the history of ACs can arguably stretch right back to biblical times as exemplified in the bible[xii] when Gideon ran his own *AC* in order to select Israelite warriors and when God intimated that there were too many people available for the task. There is however no record that Gideon undertook any form of *CV tablet sift*, which would have course have been a heavy burden to bear.

The Second World War saw the prevalence of assessment centres in a military capacity used by both Axis and Allied sides and, in modern business settings, they are seen to be effective in predicting organisational achievement. For businesses, this is the Holy Grail of all assessment activities. Anything that has predictive qualities is, for obvious reasons, the most valuable of processes to undertake.

The structure of ACs will depend on multiple evaluations in a range of contexts that will hopefully provide corroborated data on essential competencies required for the role. Ideally, the exercises will simulate the role in question or at least elements of that role, which allows the assessment board to understand the extent to which the candidate might be suited to the job.

§

All of this makes sense and all the more so because candidates have multiple opportunities to prove themselves and potentially recover from any mishaps that might occur at any stage in the process. It is not one chance only with success or failure hinging on single activities – as you might experience with individual and more abstract tests that crop up at earlier stages in recruitment processes. And of course, the assessors generate a set of scorecards or marking sheets, which are populated with data that is comparable between candidates.

What could go wrong?

Well, just about everything, as it happens.

§

As we are now well-versed, these logically defined processes with their seemingly strong evidential outputs can be scuppered or at least skewed by the manner in which they are implemented.

Firstly, ACs are resource-heavy, which immediately puts pressure on organisations to find suitably qualified assessors to support the events. And again, as with interviews and sifting exercises, we are entering the realms of dependence upon the skills, understanding and qualification of the assessors themselves. Add to this, you have the real risk of unconscious bias or albeit on rarer occasions, conscious bias, which may act to the detriment of the candidates whether that is in the way in which exercises are run or scores recorded.

No matter how much of a more liberal country you think we are, do not be so naive to think that these biases are anything other than real and in operation in all aspects of everyday life. And that includes selection and recruitment processes. Laws tackling discrimination and prejudice many have become tighter, but the negativity still exists, ranging from prissy nimbyism to frothing hatred.

As I always say, you should not spend your time worrying about the nutters out on the street shouting and bawling. They will never achieve anything. Worry about the respectable ones, going quietly about their business every day making decisions that count. If there is warped bigotry there, that is where the damage will be done.

Prejudice has never been greater in society; it has just gone more underground. But it does not all have to be deliberate. Thinking more positively, though still in the negative sphere, of course we all have human failings, and these assessment centres require a tremendous amount of focus for assessors over a long period of time. Therefore, mistakes are ever-increasingly likely to be made.

As a candidate, the pressure to perform can be challenging and in some extreme cases debilitating. And there is very little in practice that is done to attend to such individual concerns which can be exacerbated by personal styles, difficulty in striking rapport, or how well they can cope in the presence of other dominant personalities. In my experience, assessment centres are strongly favourable to individuals with outgoing bigger personalities, and candidates are frequently scored higher when they demonstrate those traits.

§

So, you see, even with modes of assessment that are almost universally accepted for their validity and reliability, there are issues in their implementation and clear indications that candidates may not perform to the best of their ability in the eyes of the panel. Furthermore, what gets recorded and stands as an objective record of good/bad performance may be far removed from that in reality.

As a candidate, you need to be clear on any adjustments you may require, particularly if the day involves a group exercise, which for candidates with any social impairment may be a car crash waiting to happen. Never be afraid to broach the question of alternative assessments.

For other general advice, these can be very difficult assessment stages to game, but you can take some action to ensure that you are ticking some boxes, without necessarily compromising your integrity. For example, in a group exercise, no matter how difficult it may be, you need to make sure that you have voiced some valid points in the course of the discussion. It is naturally stating the obvious that if you do not say anything, they will have nothing to assess.

Thankfully on some occasions, group exercises are facilitated by one of the assessment panel, who ensures that the dominance of some personalities is somewhat moderated. Perhaps this is something you can ask about in advance of your AC if you have those concerns.

At all times if you are interacting with other people in the course of those assessments, try to make yourself more middle of the road. If you are just too loud, you are likely to be considered a pain in the arse. If you are too quiet, well, you are not going to be considered somebody who is going to make an impact when in-role.

As I have mentioned, it is certainly the case that the louder candidates generally do better, and that their raised voices can sometimes gain more points than those contributions that contain more merit. It is the extremity that is the most damaging.

§

All in all, though, far from their objective qualities that are so keenly trumpeted in the recruitment and assessment world, ACs can be as inaccurate as they are traumatic. Think about your own situation and people who work alongside you in your job and then tell me about the predictive quality of assessment centres.

You do not have to look far for justification that there must be frequent issues in their use and implementation. But getting rid of them is unlikely ever to be on the cards. They are just way too ingrained and there are just so few alternatives. In fact, I am not so sure that they are such a bad idea, but there needs to be more investment put into them and a high degree of discipline that such events are not run unless stringent criteria are met in terms of available and trained resources.

In the meantime, though, be very careful indeed.

20 – Is it Offer, Nothing?

Post-selection retention – Offers and Onboarding

The world of *offers and onboarding* or *O&O* reflects one of those delightful blends of fact and fiction that will be familiar to anybody, whatever their taste in organisationally stimulated entertainment might be.

In terms of fact, as a successful candidate, you will of course have received an offer.

The fiction often begins when the question of *onboarding* arises. This is the process also known as *organisational socialisation*, whereby a new employee can acquire the knowledge, skills and behaviours that will enable them to become an effective member of that organisation. It is a process of familiarisation with organisational norms. Sounds absolutely brilliant in theory and a welcome bridge for outsiders to navigate what can be a tricky path to the inside of an organisation. If you like, the mechanism that allows people to hit the ground running, at least to an extent, or to prevent them from falling through the gaping chasms in the floor.

It is certainly the case for organisations that a poor onboarding process can be hugely costly, in that it might lead to poor performance and higher turnover levels. Indeed, there are indications, gleaned from innumerable sources, that up to one-third of new hires quit their jobs within the first 90 days. One of the issues with onboarding is that it is seen by employees as just another box to be ticked on HR's to-do list. Now whether you will have an effective onboarding process will of course depend on the organisation you are joining. However, as a candidate, you need to be aware of the level of onboarding that is likely to be in place before you accept your offer. Failure to do so may mean that you are left high and dry in your new company, without any guidance or support during what is possibly one of the most challenging periods of employment.

§

So, first of all, my suggestion would be that you include questions on onboarding to the plethora of probes that you will doubtless posit at an interview before you even get to the offer stage. This will at least demonstrate in the first instance to the hiring managers that you are engaged in the application process, to the point where you see yourself as a potential employee of the organisation. Candidates who are not engaged do not give such matters their consideration as in truth, they do not in their heart of hearts see the application progressing.

Frequently they will be ambivalent about this anyway, given the numbers game they will probably be playing, in making multiple applications in order to snag at least something that will fly for them.

One of the supreme ironies of recruitment processes is that disinterested, or at least uncommitted candidates, can get to the latter stages of processes, particularly ones loaded with online tests, only to withdraw or bomb at the interview. Then everybody loses out.

If the responses from a hiring manager to such queries are bland or not detailed, this may set alarm bells ringing because the person looking to fill a vacancy should be playing an integral role in providing inputs for the process. You may, for example, wish to ask whether or not there might be a *buddy* for you during your early days, or whether there is any assistive technology in place to provide a virtual introduction in advance of your start date (online profiles and photos of colleagues etc).

Now these are just a couple of suggestions. But if the response to any queries on this subject is that you get short shrift from the new boss, that might be the juncture at which to consider bailing out. Not only is it essential to have things in place to bridge the most difficult transition during your employment, but above all you will need the support and attention from your line manager, otherwise you are effectively gearing up to set sail on a pirate ship, where you will, without doubt, conclude your stay by walking the plank.

§

Particular care needs to be taken if parts of the recruitment process at the O&O stage are being managed by an RPO. In fact, to rewind somewhat, I would suggest that the involvement of an RPO is always established at the point of application. Of course, you can always ask a direct question though posing this out of the blue might seem a little awkward for you. One way in which you can check the existence of their involvement is by perusing the *Data Privacy Statement (or DPS)* at the start of any online application form. If they have a finger in the pie, it is there that you will see it in black and white.

Once you are aware of the involvement of an RPO this is useful information to have in the back of your mind when you are positioning or framing some of your interactions. As far as the O&O situation is concerned, you need to be concerned with two main areas.

Firstly, you need to be mindful of any personal or sensitive information you are uploading for their review. Be aware that RPOs frequently use the services of offshore providers, so at the point you are uploading your data, you cannot be sure exactly who is handling it. And that is in spite of statements contained in *DPS*, which may well confirm that none of your personal sensitive data will leave the EU. It is a much safer proposition to provide this documentation only to named sources within the HR teams of prospective employers once you have confirmed their identity. While this may sound like overkill, please give it some consideration. But at the end of the day, it is your data, and you will be the decision-maker on how it should be handled and processed.

Secondly, as a candidate, you will need to appreciate that staff within an RPO will likely not ever have visited the premises of their clients, let alone have detailed knowledge or a sense or feeling for what it will be like for you as an employee on the first day with your new company. Any information they give you will likely have been provided to them in a briefing pack, the ongoing validity of which is probably to not be again verified for months on end, if ever.

Therefore, if you are led down the road where an RPO adviser is handling your onboarding, please ensure that you make firm and clear contact with the hiring organisation's HR team or better still, the hiring manager so that you can be sure that all arrangements that you need will be in place.

Again, while this may seem a little awkward for you proactively to raise this, it is better to feel some discomfort at this stage than have to deal with gaps in your onboarding when you are, for want of a better expression, landed in it. At that stage, you will have to accept whatever you are given and get on with it. You will not have any comeback or redress, apart from perhaps being reminded that it was always your responsibility to ensure that you flagged any concerns. You will also find that the more senior the position you are in, the less sympathy you get. Indeed, raising concerns at a later date may even be construed as a weakness on your part.

Not the ideal first impression to make when you are newly on the job.

Just be mindful that whenever you raise a concern with a recruiter, however strong your case is, your own conduct, responsibilities and adherence to the process will come under close scrutiny first.

They call it survival and make no mistake that, if there is a choice for someone to be thrown under the bus, the volunteer is you. Every time.

These onboarding processes are always going to be tricky, simply by virtue of the fact that in most companies the recruiting left hand does not know what the operational right hand is doing.

Throw an RPO into the equation – with an RPO adviser who is simply processing a transaction and who has no sympathy or empathy for you – and as a candidate, you will be a further step again removed from organisational reality. Never assume that these matters will be attended to and laid on for you. You have to grasp the nettle and get yourself onto the front foot.

21 – Food for Fraught

Through different lenses – candidate feedback

Let us first acknowledge that for candidates, this is the one element in a recruitment process where candidates will get bent out of shape and self-flagellated into a frenzy.

For them, the question of feedback, particularly after being rejected, is felt to be critical. Now this should not pose too much of a challenge for assessors after an interview, at least in terms of actually having something to say.

As you may well imagine, feedback after CV sifts is very rarely offered, and even if requested will garner a response that is practically useless. In most cases, no response would even be given at all, and it is not difficult to understand why. Most of the time, there would not have been any real evidential basis on which to reject your application in the first instance. In these cases, the less that is said the better. Partly because organisations do not wish to give potentially litigious candidates a hook onto which they would like to hang their tribunal (or even time-and-resource-sucking) hat.

When they do offer some scraps to the candidate, they will be very careful to couch it in terms of, *'The panel felt that on the day...'* in order to express that any rejection is not an absolute dismissal of the individual but just a snapshot of what was said or done on that day only. And as I have previously noted, it is always a *regret*, never a *rejection*.

Nobody wants to say anything that they cannot back up with facts and at the same time, nobody wants to jab the hornets' nest. Well, not directly, anyway.

While everything purports to be an objective assessment, the words will always be about distancing everybody from a commitment to exactly that. No wonder people do get antagonised. While the words may have been softened, the candidates will still see what they understand to be the disingenuity of it all.

In practice though, even at ACs, a lot of organisations are struggling to provide meaningful feedback. In fact, for the same reasons. A lot of the time, they are simply making their decisions on perception, or it may well be that you have undertaken an interview or AC when a decision to hire an internal candidate has already been made. Your attendance at the latter stage may well simply have been window dressing. It is by no means a rare occurrence.

From my own personal experiences, I have found some interviewers almost shamelessly transparent unless they of course did not realise that what they were telling me was plainly absurd. Like the time I went for an interview with an NHS organisation, which was a little bizarre as one of the interview panel was the *Payroll Manager* – even though this was for a *Head of Recruitment* role and therefore entirely unrelated. When I was later contacted to tell me I had been unsuccessful, the hiring manager helpfully suggested that the panel had a concern that I would not be able to 'hit the ground running' because I had not any experience of having worked within the NHS during my career. Clearly, that was something that they could have ascertained upon reading my CV before taking the decision to invite me to interview, but what have I said about CV sifts? Great to have been invited, but this was a good example of when I should have been sifted out if the reasoning held up.

But hey, it garnered immediate prestige in my personal hall of fame. To have been invited to interview without my CV and application having been read, well, that was something. At the same time, to have been rejected by a panel that included the nondescript payroll droid, who had asked me, '*what had been the most unpleasant moment in my career*': *P*riceless.

> *Sitting opposite a useless clown like you for sixty minutes, I should think.*

Thought it. Wished I had said it.

§

That was not my only encounter with the provision of dross feedback.

I also received some true gems from a local government assessment process that confirmed my presentation to the panel had been thorough and excellent, I had answered all their questions effectively, and to boot my answers contained a lot of detail.

Answers with a lot of detail? What was I thinking? Apparently, it was too much information for the panel to digest. It is true, I did try to answer the questions fully.

The hiring manager then went on to say that he thought, himself, that a lot of detail was actually better than answers that contained very little information and then returned to the previously cited as excellent presentation to raise a couple of negatives.

Eh? So, from excellent to having some negatives in the space of sixty seconds. What gems was this spunkoid lickspittle about to impart?

Well firstly, I had exceeded the maximum ten slides permitted even though I pointed out that slides number one and twelve were a title slide and a slide simply stating *Thank You*, respectively.

In my book, essential top-and-tail components of a professional presentation but not sensible to include them as part of the ten slides and leave out 20% of the content. He also mentioned that he had to hurry me along towards the end of the presentation, which demonstrated a concern for the panel about my time management!

I have to say I found all of this rather amusing because the person leading the panel had stated at the start of the presentation that he would signal to me when there was one minute to go. And which of course he himself did not do.

But back to my feedback which I was at this stage quite enjoying. The poor chap then further added that the successful candidate had had extensive line management experience, having been a team leader at the very same organisation for a number of years. At that point, I smelled the sweet faint odour of an *internal hire* and the growingly inescapable conclusion that I had never been in the races from the off.

Particularly as my CV clearly had outlined a twenty-year-plus history of line management that had culminated in positions, might I say, at a higher level than this particular hiring manager themselves, not to mention a barely post-fledgling team leader?

At the end of the day, it looked like they had simply got a free piece of consultancy from me through my presentation on which they had few questions to put to me in the aftermath. So, bollocks to them. At least it made the rejection more palatable in a way, and I am not sure – in all honesty – that I would have been a great hire for their organisation anyway. What I saw during the interview did suggest that it might all have ended in tears.

What did nevertheless make me laugh was that this was an organisation that was recruiting someone to oversee a digital transformation project and then take over as a *Service Director* once that program had concluded. Now whether it would be me or somebody else, it certainly was not going to be a suitable job for a *Team Leader* with just a handful of years' experience as a first-line manager.

But that is the crazy bizarre world of recruitment and the desire to pander to the path of least resistance and the lure of internal candidates. With hindsight, and that kicked in relatively quickly after exiting that building, it was always going to be a case of *better out than in* for that job.

And that is because it was going to be a toughie even for someone with twenty-five years and a host of other digitisation projects behind them. Wow, this one was going to burn and by all accounts was starting to shake 2 months in. But you cannot tell them, these people in their little ivory towers. They think they know it all and often know *jack*.

Well, they have certainly added something to their collective experience now.

My message to you, the candidate, is that you just need to step back after a disappointment and reflect. Think about what's happened, isolate the facts, and reflect.

After that job, I was momentarily disappointed not to get it, but the more I reflected, the more I realised that they were the screwed-up ones and the ones who ended up shafting themselves with their own stupidity.

Yes, you will muck up a few interviews yourself, no doubt. But a lot of the time you will realise it's not you, *it's them*.

§

But let us just revert to the question of feedback and the *Psycho Matrix*.

Feedback on psychometric tests is a slightly different kettle of fish. There are a couple of reasons for this.

Firstly, psychometric tests are designed in such a way that they incorporate anti-faking measures so that the test is always testing ability and not what the candidate says because they think that that is what the test administrator wants to hear. With these tests, even the recruiter will not know precisely which questions the candidate got right, and which questions the candidate got wrong.

It is obvious why this is shrouded in mystery because the test suppliers do not want to divulge the correct answers, which candidates will then subsequently learn for application on later tests. It is about maintaining the integrity of the tests. There may all the same be some automatically generated summary reports from test suppliers, which may give some indication of the candidates' strengths. So, these may say that in a *critical reasoning test*, for example, a candidate scored high in *recognising assumptions* but lower in *drawing conclusions*.

And of course, this feedback will always be relative to the performance of a comparator group. It is never a question of saying that the candidate scored a certain number of marks out of 15 for example, but that the candidates concerned scored at a particular percentile in relation to candidates of a similar level who also took the test. Like other *senior managers* or *accountants* who took the test, for example.

Test suppliers and recruiters will see this type of feedback as being useful because it highlights, at a high level, performance areas on which candidates need to work so that they are best placed to pass a test, whatever that may be, at a point in the future. In the case of overall percentile comparisons, this will not help the candidate in terms of their development but will at least give them an indication of where they sit in comparison with a wider field. The feedback therefore achieves a goal of providing candidates with helpful indicators while maintaining the integrity of the test.

That should be well received by candidates then? Well, actually, no.

This is because when candidates are asking for feedback, they are actually implicitly posing a very different question. They are looking for information that will help them pass the test next time round. It is not about development because most candidates absolutely believe that they are the right person for the job and that the tests that they are required to face are an obstacle to overcome and in effect, an occupational hazard. They simply want the key to the door. This divergence of perspective is why the question of feedback is always a tricky one for recruiters and candidates to tap dance around.

In the same way that many recruiters have lost sight of the purpose of an assessment exercise, so have a lot of candidates.

For the recruiters, it is about placements and money and certainly not about attracting great talent and ensuring that that great talent has every opportunity to progress through a fair and scientific process resulting in the objective decision to hire or to reject.

For the candidates, it is frequently about navigating the tricky hurdles of an obstacle course in order to achieve the prize of the job rather than approaching an assessment exercise with confidence in the knowledge that they are good enough to deal with whatever is thrown at them.

Now that seems like a quite dismissive perspective on both recruiters and candidates. But having worked on both sides of the fence, I can absolutely see why candidates get off on the wrong foot. And is for one reason only. It is because recruiters, in most cases though not all, are in control of decisions and outcomes that have the most impact on the lives of those putting themselves forward as candidates. Candidates themselves have no choice other than to play the game whose rules are dictated by the people wielding the power.

As the apocryphal words of Jean-Paul Sartre go: *In a bent society nobody is straight.*

If recruiters have compromised the logic of assessment processes to such an extent that people need to step away from their own intuition and rational analysis; and if candidates feel compelled to behave differently or bizarrely in order simply to participate as recognised stakeholders; what should we expect?

Should we expect anything else than actions or behaviour that seem out of place when observed by an independent third party?

And yes, it does seem a little incongruent for me to make the confident point on maintaining the integrity of a process by not providing specific feedback on test performance when the test would have been used as it was. Namely, contrary to expert advice on the premise that hit has excluded people of insufficient ability, whereas in fact those excluded may well have demonstrated ability in one area that was good enough for the job concerned. Remember the use of online ability tests in practice?

The bottom line is that the process of assessing candidates in recruitment exercises up and down the country is fundamentally flawed. Not only that but the dialogue between candidates and recruiters is built on entirely false premises that damage brands and kill confidence. And by *confidence*, I mean not just belief and trust in organisations and their processes, but also internal personal confidence in the minds of generations of people who see opportunities snatched away by the corrupt.

§

Heavy stuff, eh? Looks like my invitation to speak at next year's CBI conference has evaporated into scented vape. But this exercise in looking at recruitment is about calling out for what it is. Until everybody gets their heads around the broken-down components of what is happening in the world of recruitment, we are never going to get our heads into a better space. And this is not the literary equivalent of everybody heading to the yoga mats, it is just about getting people to take a step back and to look to re-evaluate.

And hopefully to encourage those who are downtrodden, possibly even by their own frustrations and perceived limitations, to get back onto the front foot.

The subject of feedback will always be problematic for recruiters. It is just too tricky to provide something meaningful, without compromising their future testing activity. It is furthermore not cost-effective to spend time on individual candidate records in order to draw out something specific and useful. That is why it is always general and high-level – often now automated – which candidates find rather less than useless.

Of course, as noted, candidates generally seek feedback on how to pass tests rather than how to develop and it is always going to be a challenge when feedback and scores cannot be *proved* with reference to answer keys.

For reasons we have examined, that is not going to change.

So that is, I am afraid, as far as test feedback will ever go. Recruiters will tick the box when they do provide it, candidates will remain dissatisfied.

On the positive side, at least these recruiters are providing something. Many do not even bother and all you will be left with is a bland, templated email of regret.

With feedback, it will always be about what you regard as the lesser of two evils.

Endnote

Thank you for taking the time to read this book and I hope you have gained some useful insights from it. As noted in the introduction, it was never my intention to provide a technical manual on recruitment. Such books already exist in the marketplace and cover the subject most adequately.

I hoped primarily to reflect that common recruitment processes in practice do not reflect their most ostensible purpose. To me, they are hypocritical and duplicitous, to the extent that businesses and candidates suffer while only the recruiters win.

Whether by luck or judgement, you will end up being *freaking hired* or *freaking rejected*. The *flypaper* motif for outsourced contact centres might equally be applied to the recruitment agencies and functions you will encounter wherever you go.

And make no mistake, there are *freaks* at the helm in whatever direction you turn.

More egregious still, they kill opportunity. In a society that strives to eradicate inequality through the promotion of opportunity, these recruitment practices serve to subjugate people and support existing mechanics of inequality.

In the wider society, where you have extremist factions that seek to act to the detriment of minority groups, the righteous take issue with that and act decisively to prevent it. This all sounds fine and dandy to me if we are intending to protect the equality of man.

Now I am not saying that an unfair recruitment process in practice is on a par with fascism. Well, some elements might be, if direct discrimination comes into play, but that is not the point I am making. What I am saying is that any processes that deliver the same outcome that a blatantly discriminatory action would seek to achieve are converging on the same long-term objectives as those who deliberately promulgate injustice. It is not necessarily the case that these objectives are intended, and I believe they are largely the by-product of an imbalanced focus on cost saving and efficiency that is a wholly false economy.

But if they achieve the same result, we should be fighting them with the same vigour as we seem more prepared to do when questionable activities happen more openly.

One issue with recruitment appears to be the normalisation of the madness. We all seem to have buckled up our braces and got on with it, upper lips stiffened. As the satirist Kurt Tucholsky (and indeed allegedly Stalin) once said, '*One death is a catastrophe; a hundred thousand deaths is a statistic*.'[xiii] Such is the prevalence and volume of recruitment misdemeanours, we have arguably desensitised ourselves from their individual and personal impact and allowed them to wash over us like a fact of life that we should simply and unquestioningly accept.

I hope that in reading this book, it will all now start to be questioned, and not just in ephemeral outbursts after rejection.

A usurpation does not need to be violent to still deprive you of your freedoms. It doesn't even need to be a coup and happen in an instant.

For me, anything that limits opportunity equates to one element of society usurping another. It is a way of permanently shifting goal achievement to some sections of society over others. Not necessarily intentionally in order to achieve those specific goals, but that is the end result.

And stupidity and our inertia will be the underlying forces that will facilitate this and seal our collective fate. Not to mention subjecting us to the stupidity of others on-going. It needs to be challenged.

But recruitment enterprises continue to entrench themselves further in their fallacies by neither learning lessons from their own missteps nor those of others.

Recruiters who claim to champion great talent and promote diversity sound like those who promise to stop the beatings when morale improves. They do as much as anyone to maintain the status quo of inequality. Remember the words of Foucault at the start of this book: (...) *what they do not know is what what they do does*.

At least for this, we would credit them with only *amorality* which is arguably an improvement on the *immorality* they show in doing what they do in the first instance.

But even notwithstanding intent, it rarely fails to amaze how recruitment organisations can demonstrate such self-confounding positions and an essential lack of savvy. Effortlessly slipping into upscaled activity, taking advantage of volume technologies and assuming that what was once a very personable process could be run at scale with no significant challenges.

If you look around in all areas of society, the very growth that businesses see as the sign of success will very often be the factor that ruins them. Look how large companies have struggled with customer service delivery, which was always the cornerstone of the smaller business success story.

Recruitment has gone the same way.

They want money and more of it through volume but have forgotten that they are dealing with people. They think that the way they conduct their business reflects progress, but they are killing the confidence in their brands. Change will only happen when they see the gaps on their bottom line. And already there is a shift in perception.

A number of the cocksure new boutique agencies that have sprung up in city centres around the country are starting to fold. Clients just do not trust them – and neither do candidates. The bell has however not yet fully tolled; it is merely a chime.

Maybe the directors of these now-defunct hubs who have been forced to re-enter as employees in more mainstream agencies will carry the lessons back into the industry and generate change. But you know, I cannot help feeling that they will simply fall back into their old ways of chasing money, *route one*.

Those in denial at the current state of recruitment will point to their CIPD qualifications and their process manuals as evidence of their professionalism and conscientiousness. But it has not always been about poor processes or the lack of processes – though undoubtedly both feature.

It is largely the result of the ineffective performance of individuals, who are tasked with implementing what are, to the outsider, seemingly robust processes. The micro-detail of a misplaced action that can torpedo something set down with the best of intentions. It is very easy to take any activity wildly off-course through the slimmest of misinterpretations while still returning documentation that reflects validity and reliability. And in many cases, it is never uncovered.

Of course, the supreme irony is that there is a self-perpetuating cycle at work. The very people who subvert recruitment processes in practice – albeit unintentionally - are those who were themselves recruited in similar contexts.

The lunatics really are running the asylum.

So, while I have not been able to provide all the answers in terms of how to sidestep the nonsense of recruitment malpractice, I hope I have been able to provide enough useful pointers that will help to keep you on the front foot.

I am indeed hoping that I will have brought forth sufficient tips to help stymie the progress of dishonesty and deception, so you can salvage your opportunities.

But most of all I wanted to shine a light behind the familiar scenes you will inevitably encounter. In doing so, I hope you will be able to digest the real backdrop, internalise, and gain clarity.

A string of rejections from these clowns does not equate to failure.

Yes, you will flunk a few – we all make mistakes and that is a fact of life and a fact of the human condition. But do not let these bastards get you down. Everybody has a niche, and everybody has some value to give. You just need to find the ones who will appreciate yours.

While the quest continues, rise above the mayhem, and see that very often *it is not you, it is them.* You will not regret it.

Just remember the words attributed to Jean-Paul Sartre that offer the best advice to anybody dealing with the challenges of identifying the best first step after rejection:

'Freedom is what you do with what's been done to you'.

Good luck.

Notes

[i] https://www.amazon.co.uk/dp/B07SWH9MFF

[ii] In a letter to Oskar Pollack (1904)

[iii] Sartre, J. P. THE FLIES (1943) act 3, sc. 2

[iv] Foucault quoted in Dreyfus, H.L. and Rabinow, P. (1983) *Michel Foucault: Beyond Structuralism and Hermeneutics.* 2nd edn. p187 Chicago: University of Chicago Press

[v] McKinsey Quarterly 3(3):44-57 · January 1998

[vi] https://ptc.bps.org.uk/information-and-resources/information-testing/guidelines-testing-and-test-use

[vii] https://www.gov.uk/guidance/equality-act-2010-guidance

[viii] https://www.gov.uk/employment-appeal-tribunal-decisions/the-government-legal-service-v-ms-t-brookes-ukeat-0302-16-rn

[ix] Larkin, P. *This Be the Verse*, from *Collected Poems* (Farrar Straus and Giroux, 2001) Copyright © Estate of Philip Larkin

[x] Habermas, J. (1962), *The Structural Transformation of the Public Sphere: An Inquiry into a Category of Bourgeois Society.* Translated by Thomas Burger and Frederick Lawrence, MIT Press (1989)

[xi] "Schools serve the same social functions as prisons and mental institutions- to define, classify, control, and regulate people". from *Discipline and Punish*, Michel Foucault (1975)

[xii] Judges 7: 4-7

[xiii] Tucholsky, K. (1932) "*Der Tod eines Menschen: das ist eine Katastrophe. Hunderttausend Tote: das ist eine Statistik!*". Lerne Lachen Ohne Zu Weinen Section: Französischer Witz (French Wit), Start Page 147, Quote Page 148, Ernst Rowohlt Verlag, Berlin, Germany. First published 1925)

www.ingramcontent.com/pod-product-compliance
Lightning Source LLC
Chambersburg PA
CBHW030611220526
45463CB00004B/1249